Deep Prayer

Deep Prayer
Healing for the Hurting Soul

Paul DeBlassie III

Foreword by John Sanford

CROSSROAD • NEW YORK

1990

The Crossroad Publishing Company
370 Lexington Avenue, New York, N.Y. 10017

Copyright © 1990 by Paul DeBlassie III

Printed in the United States of America

Library of Congress Cataloging-in-Publication Data

DeBlassie, Paul.
 Deep prayer : healing for the hurting soul / Paul DeBlassie.
  p.   cm.
  ISBN 0–8245–1016–X
  ISBN 0-8245-1058-5 (pbk)
  1. Prayer.   I. Title.
BV215.D35   1990
248.3′2—dc20   89–48895
                                                            CIP

To Kathy—
". . . and now we see!" (John 9:25)

Contents

Foreword

When I learned from Paul DeBlassie that he was writing a book on prayer I awaited its publication with keen anticipation. I knew Dr. DeBlassie to be a Christian with a strong faith and a psychologist skilled in working with people on a deep level. I believed that a book he might write on prayer would contain much knowledge and wisdom as well as being filled with faith. I hoped for a book that would give healthful spiritual food to those Christians among us who are not willing to give up their Christian faith to a secular world, but are not helped by simplistic answers to life's difficult questions; those who have to find their own individual way as Christians and their own way of experiencing God. When I read *Deep Prayer* I was not disappointed.

The title of the book, *Deep Prayer*, arouses one's interest and curiosity. I found myself waiting for a definition of this "deep prayer" but a succinct definition does not emerge. Although Dr. DeBlassie says many things about deep prayer, no neatly phrased definition is forthcoming. But as I progressed through the book I realized that the meaning of deep prayer was in fact unfolding before me. I was not being *told* what it was, I was being *shown* what it was. I was being led into an understanding of the nature of deep prayer in a way that satisfies the soul as well as the intellect. For what Dr. DeBlassie means by deep prayer cannot be understood by digesting a rational definition; its meaning must be absorbed by living the kind of life from which deep prayer emerges. As the word "deep" implies, this kind of prayer comes up from deep within us. It is prayer that emerges from an in-depth way of spiritual life. It is more a living process than a technique. It develops from a life of depth, a life in which God becomes increasingly a reality to us as we become deep people, people who express themselves effectively in outer life as they deepen their inner life.

Dr. DeBlassie's book made me reflect on the soul, which is our inner depth. Like deep prayer, the word "soul" cannot be defined to

our satisfaction, but it can be described, and as we describe the soul
we become increasingly aware of her. Most of modern psychology
knows nothing of the soul. An examination of a modern dictionary
of psychology will not have the word in it. And yet the very word
"psychology" means the "study of the soul." For our word "soul" is
the English translation of the Greek word *psyche.* Thus psychology
should be the "logos," that is, the study of the soul, but since psychology is so largely dominated by a materialistic attitude the soul is
disregarded. So the very word "soul" has all but vanished from our
language, and the soul herself is regarded as a relic, an antiquated
notion that has no place in a scientific and rational world. In our
modern world we like to suppose that we are "done with soul," finished with her—though not quite, for the word "soul" is a stubborn
one. It hangs on and almost involuntarily we find ourselves using it
because no other word expresses what the word "soul" expresses. So
we say of a certain singer that she has something called "soul," or of
a person that he has "soulful eyes," or of a dispirited person that he
has "lost his soul."

In antiquity the soul was an important idea. We find it prevalent
among the ancient Greeks. In its Hebrew form (*nephesh*) it occurs
well over four hundred times in the Old Testament. In the New Testament it is on virtually every page. There we learn that every individual has a soul, and that to lose one's soul is to lose one's life, for
the body dies if the soul leaves it. A quaint idea? And yet today
in psychosomatic medicine we learn that when that-within-us-which-
wants-to-live (soul) ceased to care, the body does sicken and die. We
also learn from the New Testament that when two or more people are
close to one another in friendship and love they then "share one
soul." The Old Testament said the same thing and spoke of the
friendship between David and Jonathan as so strong that it was as
though they shared the same soul. For the soul always speaks of
passion, of depth, of feeling, of pathos. So in Gethsemane we are told
that the soul of the Lord was "sorrowful unto death." We also find
that the soul can be won or lost; it can be made alive or it can die; it
can be strengthened or corrupted. We find that it is of inestimable
value, so much so that we are admonished by the Lord not to fear
a person who can kill our body but to fear those persons who can
kill our souls (by exerting a negative and seductive influence upon
us). For the soul is also a battleground. Forces of creativity and
forces of evil compete for control of the soul. The first way leads

to life, the second way to that spiritual death which is spoken of in the fourth Gospel. And lastly we learn that the soul when made alive in this life lives on in the next life, not as a disembodied spirit, but with its own spiritual body, going into a life to come that escapes the ability of our earthly imagination to picture.

I believe the reader of *Deep Prayer* will find that the soul is touched and responds to Dr. DeBlassie's message. For the deep prayer of which he speaks comes from the soul and is medicine for the soul. Those who wish to be spoon-fed with a spiritual talk that fits into their preconceived ideas may find this book difficult, but for those who are willing to dig deeper, to go into soul herself, there will be rich rewards.

JOHN SANFORD

1

God Is Bigger
Than Your Biggest Problem

Now to him who by the power at work within us is able to do far more abundantly than all that we ask or think. . . . (Eph. 3:20)

God is bigger than your biggest problem. When confronted with the enormity of life's difficulties and challenges, we often succumb to feeling overwhelmed and powerless. The fact of the matter is that a power lies within each individual to deal with and overcome the most potent negative forces that attempt to thwart, attack, and injure human life. That power is God.

Through deep prayer, the inspirational power and healing required for positive daily living can be discovered in the depths of the soul, wherein resides God. Deep prayer is that encounter with the holy presence of God that leaves the soul filled with a sense of awe. In this a person knows that he or she has contacted the living presence of Jesus. The heart and mind feel transformed, renewed, and rejuvenated. Real prayer is deep prayer, an experience that fills the soul with the love of God.

In the words of an Eastern saint,

Sometimes from prayer, a certain contemplation is born which makes prayer vanish from the lips. And he to whom this contemplation happens becomes as a corpse without soul, in ecstasy. This we call sight during prayer, and not an image or form forged by fantasy. . . . Also in this contemplation . . . there are degrees and differences in gifts. But till this point there is still prayer. For thought has not yet passed into the state where there is no prayer, but to a state superior to it. For the motions of the tongue and the heart during prayer are keys. What comes after them is the entering into the treasury. Here, then, all mouths and tongues are silent, and the heart, the senses, the daring spirit, that swift

1

bird, and all their means and powers and the beseeching persuasions have to stand still there: for the Master of the house has come.

The treasure that this Eastern saint speaks of is deep prayer. Here the soul meets the Master of the house. God is encountered, rational faculties are suspended, and the soul is elevated to a knowledge of and union with the love of God. Divine contemplation transcends earthly problems and yet empowers the individual to resolve the greatest of practical difficulties with the very wondrous power of Him who is able to do immeasurably more than all we ask or imagine, according to His power that is at work within us.

I remember a haggard, poorly dressed, worried-looking seventeen-year-old boy telling me about the misery that plagued him. As he sat in the large earth-toned, cushioned chair in my consulting room, waves of pain came forth from his soul. In just seventeen years of life, he had felt enough agony to last two lifetimes. The tone of his voice seemed hollow as he described his family life. When he was only nine years of age, his mother died. In his words, "I felt like my whole world came to an end. She was the one person that I knew really loved me. And now she was gone."

Although he was physically present with me in the consulting room, I felt as though he were miles and miles away from me. The pain of losing his mother at an early age, together with feeling isolated from his father and other family members, caused him to retreat deep within himself. By cutting himself off from his feelings and from people, he hoped to insure himself against the pain of further loss.

The years that followed were packed with severe emotional and spiritual trauma. An ostensibly sensitive and understanding uncle successfully maneuvered himself into a position of trust and confidence. He then exercised his influence in a cunning and cruel manner. He gradually seduced and repeatedly sexually abused the boy.

After running away from the uncle's home and sleeping behind bushes, under boxes in alleyways, and beneath layers of old newspapers near trash bins, he was arrested and placed in a detention facility for incorrigible children. He quickly learned to hide his feelings, act tough, and do what was needed to get by. He felt more and more alone, unloved and angry.

One day, after classes at the detention facility had been dismissed, he was approached by a rather young and compassionate-looking

man. This caring man candidly and forthrightly told the young boy
that he would like to get to know him. He had evidently been watching this boy for a number of days through a window where visitors
were allowed to observe the teenagers and their teachers. The hard-
ened young boy scoffed and walked away from the compassionate
young man.

That evening, this young boy received another message from the
man who wanted to help him. The message read, "I would like to
help you in whatever way you need help. If you need a friend, know
that I am here. You have my permission to call me if you want to talk
with me. Enclosed you will find my card with my name and telephone number on it. If you need a friend, call me."

During the weeks that followed this teenager did, in fact, reach out
to the compassionate and understanding visitor. As a church deacon,
this sensitive man constantly ministered to those in need. He felt a
special drawing toward this incarcerated teenager. During at least a
dozen telephone visits, the deacon spoke to the troubled teenager
about the love of God, about God's desire to forgive him, and about
God's ever-ready longing to be his best friend.

One day, in coming to my office, the teenager joked about this
deacon and said, "I used to think that I knew everything. I never
thought anybody would ever want to spend time with me. I used to
feel like nobody cared about me, including God. I even thought that
this man just wanted something from me. At first I thought that he
was a joke. But when he was always there when I called him, I felt
like he really cared about me. And if he cared about me, maybe God
really loved me too."

Some six months later, this same teenager remarked, "You know,
that man really helped me. If it wouldn't have been for him telling
me that he was interested in me, I wouldn't feel better today. I never
said anything to him, but down deep I sort of knew that he did care
for me. I never showed it, but I felt good when he said he wanted to
get to know me. He wasn't like all the others who had hurt me.
Because of him, I started to feel better toward people. Pretty soon, I
even started to feel better about God. I think I know now that God
does love me and that He's not out to hurt me."

Some months after being visited by the deacon who befriended
him, this young boy was placed in a foster home. One night, he
awoke with a start at 3:00 A.M. He was covered with perspiration
and filled with terror. He felt utterly and completely alone in a cold

and hostile world. His heart pounded. His breathing was rapid and shallow. His soul cried out for someone to turn to for help.

With great moaning and travail of spirit he pled that if God did, in fact, exist He would come to him at that very moment. He sought relief from inner torment. With complete yieldedness, he implored One whom he did not know for compassion and healing.

He recounted to me, "All of a sudden, I sensed a presence in my room. It was as if someone I could not see or hear, someone I could only feel, was with me. I felt quiet all over. I almost forgot where I was. I had no sense of feeling bad. I only felt warm and good inside. I knew everything was going to be all right."

This divine encounter was preceded by an act of simple human kindness that, on the surface, had not even been acknowledged but yet was deeply impactful. One can be predisposed to an encounter with God by having first encountered human charity. Genuine human love readies the soul for the embrace of God.

The sensing of the divine presence is the most common manifestation and confirmation of deep prayer. It soothes the body, mind, and spirit. Once the human soul enters deeply into God, all facets of life are positively affected.

The *Medical Tribune* recently reported the beneficial effects of prayer. Cardiologist Dr. Randy Byrd arranged for people around the country to pray intensely daily for 192 coronary care-unit patients at San Francisco General Hospital. In this highly controlled and experimental study, a total of 393 coronary patients were studied. Those patients in the "prayed-for" group had from five to seven people in the country praying for them each day. The other 201 patients in the control group did not receive any sort of intercessory prayer.

This study was conducted over a ten-month period. All the patients were considered to be statistically comparable in age and severity of condition. Those involved in intercessory prayer were given the name of the patient, the diagnosis and condition of the patient, and were asked to pray for "beneficial healing and quick recovery" for each person.

In analyzing the results, Dr. Byrd discovered that the "prayed-for" patients manifested significantly fewer complications in the coronary-care unit. Only three of the "prayed-for" patients required antibiotics, compared with sixteen in the control group. Six "prayed-for" patients suffered pulmonary edema, while eighteen in the other group experienced that particular complication. None of the patients that received prayer needed intubation, while twelve of the unprayed-for patients required this procedure.

The doctors who were informed of the results of the study agreed that prayer can be efficacious in promoting physical health and well-being. One doctor noted, "Now I pray for my own patients, and I feel my prayers benefit them." Another cardiologist said., "I believe that patients who are named in prayer do better."

In this case, deep prayer stirred the souls of the doctors. They had a desire now to pray for their patients, with the belief that such prayer could be beneficial. Deep prayer is indeed contagious.

Impassioned for God

Deep within the human soul stirs passion for the living God. It may be consciously denied, but the desire, indeed the hunger to know God, innately dwells in the heart of each man and woman. This passion tugs at the human heart until it is satisfied.

In the words of Dr. Carl Jung,

> The spiritual appears in the psyche also as an instinct, indeed as a real passion. . . . it is not derived from any other instinct, but is a principal "sui generis," a specific and necessary form of instinctual power.

Psychological healing and wholeness accompany the experience of both human and divine love. Human love assists one in opening up to divine caring. Once a person senses even a modicum of charity from another human being, he or she gradually but surely entrusts himself or herself to the loving embrace of God. The human soul is thus satisfied and healed.

Psychologist Dr. David McClelland of Harvard University has discovered that love and caring heal both the human soul and the body. Students were shown a film on Mother Theresa of Calcutta. This film portrayed Mother Theresa as a very compassionate and caring individual who ministered to the poor on the streets of Calcutta. The results of the research indicated that not only did the students feel an inspiration of love and caring, but that they also manifested increased signs of physical health.

Students felt great compassion and charity interiorly and, as a result, an antibody—salivary IgA—increased. This antibody provides major protection against cold and upper respiratory infection. The ability to love and care about others also seems to precipitate lower levels of the stress hormone, norepinephrine, and a higher ratio of suppressor T-cells that produce an important balance in a healthy immune system. In essence, a soul filled with love, affection, and caring may produce the side effect of a very healthy body.

Since the soul seems to hunger innately for God, it is as though the body responds affirmatively once this craving has been satisfied. The body and soul work as one. A soul in tune with God and with others is reflected in and through a healthy body. The soul and body are meant to live in God. The psalmist eloquently portrays his own passion for God:

> As a hart longs for flowing streams, so longs my soul for thee, O God. My soul thirsts for God, for the living God. When shall I come and behold the face of God? . . . Hope in God; for I shall again praise Him, my help and my God. (Ps. 42:1–2, 5)

Life is the quest of the soul in search of God—indeed, craving for God. From birth to death, the journey is meant to be one in which God is found as the pearl of great price. Nothing in all of life compares with the profound experience of sacrificing all for the sake of Christ. He and He alone is the soul's great treasure.

An allegiance to something or someone other than God, as life's primary source, infests the soul with tumultuous storms. Emotional and spiritual turmoil may reflect distance from God. The more one attempts to run away from God, the more problems may seem to plague him or her. In other words, inner discord and conflict may be projected onto the external environment in the form of chronic fighting in relationships, disaster in the work place, and personal deterioration. A person who is running away from God commonly feels like his or her life is falling apart.

Thus, a spiritually sterile life produces intense psychic misery. God alone satisfies the soul. Without Him as the fundamental, most basic relationship in life, intense misery is produced. This unhappiness is in no way of minor import. Melancholia afflicts every aspect of living for one who has drawn away from God. A soul without God is deeply miserable due to a sense of profound interior emptiness.

A soul downcast, conflicted, and empty is a soul in need of God. He alone causes the downtrodden to feel hopeful. He alone quiets the storms of personal, marital, familial conflict. He alone fills the empty heart with His own love. The crisis facing humankind is a crisis of spirituality in which the need for God and His love is surrendered to with finality.

The depth psychologist C. G. Jung further clarified the critical importance of spirituality to humankind:

> Ordinary reasonableness, sound human judgment, science as a compendium of common sense, these certainly help us over a good part of the road, but they never take us beyond the frontier of life's most commonplace realities, beyond the merely average and normal. They afford no answer to the question of the psychic suffering of a soul that has not discovered its meaning. But all creativeness in the realm of the spirit, as well as every psychic advance of man, arises from the suffering of the soul, and cause of the suffering is spiritual stagnation, or psychic sterility.

Interior pain signals an opportunity for nearness to God. Resistance merely precipitates further sickness of the soul. This pathology manifests symptoms such as anxiety, worry, dysphoria, and possibly even physical ailments. Only by satisfying one's hunger for God, through surrender, can a sense of interior ease and equanimity settle the human heart.

Jimmy, a transformed seventeen-year-old boy who had spent two years in psychotherapy, cozily sank into the large chair in my consulting office as he reflected on his newly discovered love for God. In his words, "It's like I'm all His now. I still feel scared sometimes, but when I think about Him and how He's right here with me all the time, I feel better. He's someone who will always be with me no matter what. I just feel better inside."

"Feeling better inside" describes the interior ease and soothing that accompanies the divine embrace. After much arduous searching, dryness of soul, and at times utter despair, the dawning of the realization that God loves you is as a soothing, refreshing balm to one who has been left tired, wounded, and bleeding from life's struggles. The satisfaction of meeting Him who is the source of all comfort and consolation steadies and heals the battle-scarred soul.

The Touch of Pain—The Touch of God

Tom, a sixteen-year-old teenager, suffered through his parents' divorce and was left in the custody of an emotionally distant, critical, and cold father. He recounted to me that night after night, for months on end, he ate nothing but cold beans and stale bread for dinner. His father came home too tired to cook anything else. Strewn-about beer cans, discarded containers of beans, and plastic bread bags decorated the kitchen. Each evening he opened up the can of beans, unwrapped the bread, and pulled open the pop-tops from his father's beer cans while, in the other room, his father escaped for the entire evening by watching television, program after program. In other words, Tom was, for all practical purposes, alone.

The pain of his personal loneliness exerted pressure on him to find help. He desperately needed the void within himself to be filled. He recounted to me the many paths he had trod upon searching for happiness: "I tried every drug imaginable. I sometimes smoked enough pot that I thought my brains would blow out. I took LSD. Sometimes I'd even shoot up whiskey so that I would get a quicker high. I'd get a needle full of booze, stick it in one of my veins, and shoot it in there. I'd really start flying. For a while, all of that would numb my pain. I wouldn't feel so lonely. When my high was over, I came crashing down. I felt worse off than ever. I would then try to get higher and higher. After a while, I couldn't get high enough, because I knew I was going to come down. I knew that there was no more running away."

In reflecting with me over his traumatic life, he recalled instances of sensing a loving presence. At times it felt very similar to his mother's loving presence. At other times it felt like someone or something from whom he wanted to escape. He was afraid of opening up to anyone, even a loving God.

During his first seven years, his mother would frequently tell him about his Father in heaven. She would gently encourage him to pray nightly, to worry about nothing, and to know that God loved him. As a young boy, those words were implanted in his heart. With the beginning of his mother's drug addiction and divorce from his father, he could no longer rely on the comfort of her spiritual inspiration. When he lost her he felt that God too had abandoned him.

One night, after getting drunk with some other boys in his gang, he sat alone in a dark alleyway. It was 3:00 A.M. He knew his father really didn't care. His father had probably passed out drunk early in the evening. All alone, cold and numb, Tom sat in the dark alley next to trash bins, old newspapers, and stray cats. He almost felt like crying then but would not allow himself to shed a tear. A bit of pain meant a lot of pain. He wanted no more pain, no matter what he had to do to avoid it. Little did he know that with this feeling of pain would come God's loving touch of tenderness and healing.

Crisis often inspires the experience of deep prayer. Tom felt God's touch in his life when, in a moment of desperation, he prayed, "My problems are so big God that only you can help me." He prayed this prayer during a prayer meeting with other young people present. He recalled, "All of a sudden I felt that God loved me—He really loves me!"

Great interior distress has the potential to purify one's interior being so that God's loving presence may surface. A deep blessing can be found behind the anguish and trials of life. Life provides a testing ground for men and women to decide whether they will allow themselves to be defeated by life's trials or persevere, and thus grow in self-understanding so that blessing is experienced. Under each of life's burdens, behind each painful obstacle, past each trial and test lies the pearl of great price.

As pain is rejected, God is rejected. God requires that we are completely His. This necessitates the relinquishment of old habits, behaviors, and attitudes that may feel quite comfortable. A lack of willingness to permit detachment from all else save God impedes the full absorption of God's presence. Without the pain of letting go, we are literally left without God. Great suffering paves the way for a heartfelt surrender to God.

With the embrace of pain comes surrender to the Divine. Suffering where it hurts most, in our sensitive and emotional nature, motivates us to turn toward God unconditionally. Such interior suffering propels the individual toward God in search of consolation and relief. Life's pains and hurts are quite providential, in that they cause the soul to run quickly to the Father who is the divine comforter. If this pain is ignored or deadened, as happens during intoxication, the opportunity for union with God may be missed. Suffering, especially when it hurts most, is the great enabler, motivating union with the God of all tenderness and compassion.

Thus, Jesus works in and through interior suffering. Spiritual and emotional pain need not be considered demonic. In fact, pain may superficially be regarded as a dark devil only to be later recognized as an angel of light. This light shines in our heart only when darkness has been endured.

What seems to be darkness may, in actuality, be a great and piercing light. At first, one's spiritual eyes see only darkness because the light is so blinding. Only later does the soul see clearly. Only later, after the crucifixion and death, does the disciple recognize the Lord on the Emmaus road. We see Him most clearly after times of great pain. As with all communication from God, so with pain, "You will do well to pay attention to this as to a lamp shining in a dark place, until the day dawns and the morning star rises in your hearts" (2 Pet. 1:19).

Dr. William Frye Jr., a biochemist in the psychiatry department at St. Paul–Ramsey Medical Center in St. Paul, Minnesota, researched the biochemistry of dealing appropriately with emotional pain. His hypothesis stated that emotional distress produced toxic substances in the body and that crying would help to remove them from the system. This would explain why someone who is upset or sad would feel better after having had a good cry.

In his research, Dr. Frye attempted to determine whether tears resulting from emotional distress were chemically different from tears induced by a physical irritant. The subjects watched a very sad movie and, if they were moved to weep, would catch their tears in a test tube. A number of days later, the same subjects were exposed to fresh-cut onions and their tears were again collected.

The results of the research indicated that the tears wept as the result of emotional distress and sorrow were different in chemical composition from those shed over onions. He found that emotional tears contained stress hormones. These stress chemicals were released from the body once the individual allowed himself or herself to have a good cry. Keeping feelings bottled up plugs up one of nature's most important safety valves, emotional expression in crying.

The psalmist acknowledges the torment that results from attempting to outrun interior pain as he says,

> When I declared not my sin, my body wasted away through my groaning all day long. For day and night thy hand was heavy upon me; my strength was dried up as by the heat of summer. I acknowledged my sin to thee, and I did not hide my iniquity; I said, "I will confess my transgressions to the Lord"; then thou didst forgive the guilt of my sin. . . .

Be glad in the Lord, and rejoice, O righteous, and shout for joy, all you upright in heart! (32:3–5, 11)

Emotional turmoil and groaning were deeply felt by the psalmist as he tried to maneuver out from under the heavy hand of God. In other words, heaviness of heart may be a manifestation of the presence of God. The divine light wishes to expose all that is dark. As we attempt to scurry away from this light, exhaustion and heaviness set in. Thus, a heavy heart may be a sure sign that we are trying to flee from Him who would bring healing, if we would but settle ourselves and learn what it is that the pain has to teach us.

Once the psalmist felt the full force of his interior cross, the touch of God became more light. Joy characterizes the life of one who has lived through and learned from pain. No longer did the psalmist cover up the iniquity and darkness that resided in his soul. He was created to live by and grow through God's light. Hiding in darkness, covering up his faults and sinfulness, sapped his strength. Gladness and great rejoicing filled him once he permitted himself to come face to face with the Lord of Light who alone could heal him in and through interior suffering.

A very distraught young woman once approached me seeking relief from misery and malcontent. For three years she had been under the weight of profound depression. She had sought help from doctor after doctor to no avail. She stated, "I know that you can help me. I will do anything to get better. I will allow nothing to keep me from being fully healed."

I am always a bit cautious with individuals who tell me that they have been to doctor after doctor without having received even a tidbit of solace. Typically, these individuals claim a high degree of motivation but in reality are very resistant to the process of healing. They firmly assert a willingness to do whatever is required by the psychologist, but in reality they seem to sabotage treatment every step of the way. I guided her sensitively but firmly.

I suggested that if she wished to enter in-depth psychotherapy under my care, she should begin by spending twenty minutes per day in prayer. This would prepare her soul for the spiritual journey. After thirty days of resolutely praying for twenty minutes, she could then contact me and we would arrange for our first meeting. This seemed to be a good way to test her motivation and also provide spiritual preparation for in-depth psychotherapy.

All at once she bolted up out of her chair. She exclaimed, "I can't
do that. I can't sit still with God for that long. I don't want to hear
what he has to tell me." She stormed away from me, unwilling to face
her chronic pain, unwilling to face God and her deepest self.

Yielding to purifying pain—spiritual, emotional, and physical—
heightens spiritual sensitivities to the presence of God. Pain purifies
one from preoccupation with peripheral concerns. Desires for status,
material accumulations, and recognition of various sorts fade away
during moments of interior suffering. Our intent and desires shift
from this world to the world within. For this reason, inner struggle
and pain cleanse the soul.

God's great love is most deeply encountered by those who have
suffered much, with total reliance on Him. The enormity of divine
love is apprehended only by those who surrender completely to Him.
Without complete yieldedness, the soul remains frustrated in its desire for God. Surrender brings the satisfaction of knowing Him intimately. With such divine closeness, the pains and struggles of life
draw one closer of God and thus serve as purifying agents. A great
depth of interior pain predisposes one to know the sublime sweetness
of the love of God.

St. Teresa of Avila described the paradoxical experiences of the
painful, yet sweet, divine touch:

> Our Lord was pleased that I should have at times a vision of this kind: I
> saw an angel close by me, on my left side, in bodily form. This I am not
> accustomed to see, unless very rarely. Though I have visions of angels
> frequently, yet I see them only by an intellectual vision such as I have
> spoken before. It was our Lord's will that in this vision I should see the
> angel in this wise. He was not large, but small of stature and most beau-
> tiful—his face burning as if he were one of the highest angels, who
> seemed to be all afire: they must be those whom we call cherubim. Their
> names they never tell me; but I see very well that there is in heaven so
> great a difference between one angel and another, and between those
> and the others, that I can not explain it.
>
> I saw in his hand a long spear of gold, and at the iron's point there
> seemed to be a little fire. He appeared to me to be thrusting it time and
> again into my heart, and to pierce my very entrails; when he drew it
> out, he seemed to draw them out also, and to leave me all on fire with
> the great love of God. The pain was so great that it made me moan; and
> yet so surpassing was the sweetness of this excessive pain that I could not
> wish to be rid of it. The soul is satisfied now with nothing less than

God. The pain is not bodily but spiritual; though the body has its share in it, even a large one. It is a caressing of love so sweet which now takes place between the soul and God, that I pray God of his goodness to make him experience it who may think that I am lying.

During the days this lasted I went about as if beside myself. I wished to see and speak with no one, but only to cherish my pain, which was to me a greater bliss than all created things could give me.

Thus, God transforms the most excruciating sufferings into a touch of divine love. His love permeates all that happens to us if we but have eyes to see. With an open heart, we can realize that God is speaking constantly to us about His love for us as persons. In the midst of pain He is there.

Revive the Sense of Being Led

The spiritual importance of working through personal pain can be realized once one feels the sense of being led by the Spirit of God in and through deep prayer. "For all who are led by the spirit of God are sons of God" (Rom. 8:14). The faith-assured position that God can work in and through life's tempests causes us to look beyond the immediacy of the problem and toward the finality of God's intervention and solution.

A God-directed life, rather than a circumstance-directed life, yields power to overcome the most disastrous of calamities. If God is at work in and through every circumstance, then He can always be relied upon. This necessitates that Divine Providence always be contemplated. When the external circumstance is moaned and groaned over, energy is lost and depression settles into the soul. In contrast, feeling the interior certitude that all will be well despite external circumstances is both healthy and strengthening.

St. Paul in his letter to the Romans states, "Abraham believed God, and it was reckoned to him as righteousness" (4:3). Abraham was placed in right standing with God through his faith. His belief in God's ability to help him, despite the apparent bleakness of the situation at hand, acted to imbue God's power into the problem. Once faith is released, God's power is released.

Of course, all of this depends upon the individual's willingness to follow the interior promptings of the Spirit of God. The temptation is to be controlled by a collective psychology. That is, it is often easier to follow that which is most conventional and acceptable, regardless of whether it is prompted by the Spirit of God within. Such an acquiescence to a herd psychology distances one from a personal relationship with God who dwells in the interior holy of holies. God speaks to individuals, not to herds. God is concerned about the individual human heart, not about the collective pressures of a group.

Psychological development, therefore, often entails the willingness to stand alone in faith. Such an action bespeaks a mature state of interior development and Christian faith. A person's move toward God is an individual movement that may be reflected in communal gatherings but is not dependent upon communal gatherings. Christianity, a genuine experience with God, is a matter of one person relating to one God and following His Spirit wholeheartedly and unreservedly. The sense of being led as an individual, as a precious person in His sight, is at the core of the Christian calling.

An individual must be secure with himself or herself before contentment can be found in such an intensely personal relationship with God. It often proves quite troublesome that we grow up in the constant company of others and so come to depend upon them for our happiness. Self-confidence then comes to depend upon gaining the approval of others. This obviously inhibits a deeply personal relationship with the God who requires a radical and complete yielding to Him, regardless of the opinions of others.

Only upon looking inward so as to hear His voice in the quiet of the soul can we understand both ourselves and Him better, and thus be able to interact and relate to others more constructively and creatively. In the words of one psychologist,

> Everyone has an inner and an outer self. The outer self deals with family, friends, culture, and all the other aspects of civilization. We modify and compromise the outer self to deal with the people around us. But the inner self is the true self. People in touch with their inner selves have a true sense of identity. They have a feeling of security in knowing who they really are. And by knowing their true selves, they can teach their outer self how to better interact with others.

When we find our inner selves, there we find God. He is at the deepest part of our being. As we come to know and experience Him there, our souls are nourished and contented. The fruit of this is a greater ability to love others authentically and sincerely. Being led by God into the depths of the soul eventually propels us back into the external world to relate in a caring and compassionate manner to those who are hurting.

In Christian tradition, the Desert Fathers epitomize the quest for interior holiness. During the fourth century A.D., monastic experiments had begun in the deserts of Egypt. Jerome of Antioch in 375 wrote to his friend Rufinus, "This is the outer desert where each monk remains alone in his cell . . . there is a huge silence and a great quiet there." These monks sensed the leading of God beckoning them into the desert of their own heart to encounter Him in utter simplicity.

The story is told of a holy father teaching a group of catechumens about the gospel of our Lord Jesus Christ. As he was standing on the monastery grounds, proclaiming the gospel, a peasant carrying a shovel full of sand came up, stood by him, and waited for him to finish his discourse so he could bless the sand. Once the holy father blessed the sand, the peasant hurriedly ran off. The peasant returned many times asking the holy father each time to bless the sand.

Finally the catechumens asked the holy father why the peasant was behaving in such an odd manner. He replied, "My children, I should not have boasted to you or told you about the exploits of our fathers, for fear that we should become puffed up inwardly and lose our reward. However, for the sake of your zeal and edification, because you have come so far to see us, I will not deprive you of what may be edifying, but will explain in the presence of the brethren what God in his providence has effected through us.

"The land bordering us was infertile and the peasants who owned it scarcely had a double return from the seed which they sowed, for a worm developed in the ears and destroyed the whole crop. Those farmers who had been catechized by us and had become Christians asked us to pray for the harvest. I said to them, 'If you have faith in God, even this desert sand will bear fruit for you.' Without a moment's hesitation, they filled the folds of their tunics with the sand which had been trodden by us and bringing it to me, asked me to bless it. After I had prayed that it should be done to them according to their faith, they sowed the sand together with the corn in their fields, and at once their land became extremely fertile, more than anywhere else in Egypt. As a result, it is now their custom to do this, and every year they trouble us for sand."

The lives of the Desert Fathers witnessed to the incredible power of God that can overcome the most troubling of life's problems. However, the release of such creative energy into the practicalities of daily living demands an unobstructed conduit. A soul purified of egocentric desires can be purely led by God. In this state, inner inspirations are known to be godly inspirations. A soul in this state knows such interior harmony that God's creative power flows freely, without impediment. Unreserved faith-filled interiority readies the soul to experience God's love and providence firsthand.

Reviving the sense of being led by God requires the struggle to hear His voice within. After much practice and discernment, His inspirations and touches can be clearly felt. His leading and guiding can be recognized. Being led by God, through the cultivation of much stillness and quiet, highlights in bold relief God's magnificence in contrast to the always transitory nature of everyday problems.

Essentially, then, Christianity is a faith of being impelled from within, not compelled from without. Once an individual fully enters the Christian way, the inner dimension of life becomes startlingly clear. The faith-walk is a journey within the depths of the soul. It is here, at this bottomless well, that the waters of life spring forth. It is here that spiritual thirst is quenched. From the depths of interior prayer springs forth life-giving faith.

> In hope he believed against hope, that he should become the father of many nations; as he had been told, "So shall your descendants be." He did not weaken in faith when he considered his own body, which was as good as dead because he was about a hundred years old, or when he considered the barrenness of Sarah's womb. No distrust made him waver concerning the promise of God, but he grew strong in his faith as he gave glory to God, fully convinced that God was able to do what he had promised. (Rom. 4:18–21)

Our father Abraham surely understood the inner impelling that results from authentic faith. He had been called by God to form a nation. He and his wife were childless and past the age of childbearing. Indeed, he was 100 years old, and the scriptures note that Sarah's womb was dead. Through God's miraculous intervention, he fathered a son, Isaac. His inner faith withstood the ostensibly impossible nature of his outer circumstances.

The Innermost Self

This type of genuine faith arises from the phenomena in depth psychology referred to as the self. It is that essence within each person that contains the nature of God. The self is the innermost core of our being that St. Paul describes when he prays, "that according to the riches of his glory he may grant you to be strengthened with might through his Spirit in the inner man, and that Christ may dwell in your hearts through faith . . . "(Eph. 3:16, 17).

Our inner being, or inner self, is the repository of divine creativity, energy, and fulfillment. Wayne G. Rollins in his book *Jung and the Bible* comments on the creativity of the inner self by describing it as an instinctual power that "provides the energy and sets the dream to create cities, erect cathedrals, builds bridges, plumb life's secrets, spawn the arts, and establish peace." It is the basis of all creativity.

In the words of C. G. Jung, "The inner self is a vessel filled with grace." This grace impels one to live by faith and thus be purely led by the spirit of God. Such a living faith exudes from a dynamic and vibrant relationship with a loving God who resides within the soul. Its manifestation is creative works and healthy, positive relationships.

That which is the essence of an individual, the inner self, impels one toward healing and wholeness. The self or the soul is not innately fractious. It is tranquil, whole, and creative. It participates in a transcendent relationship with God. It inspires the individual to grow toward harmony and generativity.

Quite often this movement of the soul can be sabotaged. Rather than living deeply and truthfully, the individual instead seeks a quick answer and a superficial explanation to his or her problems. This can often be noticed in individuals who want their spiritual director or psychologist to tell them what to do and how to do it. Such superficiality and withholding of truth can serve to sabotage the individual's relationship with his or her soul. Truth must be faced, no matter how painful. Inner hurt must be worked through in the depths of the soul. This alone brings healing.

Bob, a middle-aged male, described his frustration in seeking interior peace. He was ready to take the interior plunge, no matter at what cost, in order to encounter God and thus find meaning for his life. Well-meaning friends gave him a great deal of direction and advice. By the time he came to me, he said, "I am so full of everyone's advice. I have had it. Everyone has their own way of looking at things. Everyone tells me what to read. Some friends have told me steps I should take in overcoming my problem. Some have actually set up elaborate plans to help me get better. All I want is for somebody to take time to understand me. I don't care how you see things. I want you to care how I see things. I want you to understand me."

Unfortunately, many friends, doctors, and spiritual directors had tried to help this man feel better by giving him suggestions and advice. All this was to no avail. He felt enough pain and lack of meaning in life that he knew something was wrong on the inside. This spiritual pain required more than friendly advice or professional opinions. It necessitated the exploration of his soul, bringing the healing light of Jesus into the darkest recesses.

Each person has the capacity to feel the call within, inspiring him or her into a deeper relationship with God. If one listens, God's voice will indeed be heard quite clearly, a voice that calls us toward truth rather than lies, light rather than darkness, and a yielding to the natural impulsion toward God. As C. G. Jung in his book *Memories, Dreams, Reflections* wrote, "I find that all my thoughts circle around God like the planets around the sun, and are as irresistibly attracted by Him."

Elizabeth, a mother of three, had debated for two or three months before finally deciding to consult with me. She suffered from a worsening condition of anxiety. Waves of panic would flood her consciousness. She sought relief with medication, innumerable trips to the confessional, and pleading before God. Nothing seemed to work. She reported, "Finally, in desperation I prayed that God would show me how I could be helped. You came to mind. I felt that I wanted to see you."

With great reluctance she entered my consulting office. She appeared tired, haggard, and minimally motivated. As we talked, she attempted to make light of her emotional and spiritual pain. She wanted relief but was not sure how deep she was willing to go. For three months we battled her resistance.

In her words, "I knew I needed to be here. I also knew that I wanted to run away. It was as if there was this dark, deep chasm inside me. I was frightened. I knew you would help me. I just didn't know if I could go through with it. I needed to feel that God was with me. I wanted to find Him. I asked Him for a sign."

In actuality, she had prayed and asked for the intercession of St. Thérèse, the Little Flower. Just as we would ask another Christian to pray for us, so it also makes sense to ask one of the saints, already in heaven, to intercede for us, to pray for us. We are not praying to the saints. We are merely asking their intercession before God regarding our needs. In a sense, they have a more direct line of communication, since they already stand purely in His presence without the interference of this world's distractions. For this reason, she asked for the intercession of this particular saint.

Just before Elizabeth arrived at my office for her regularly scheduled appointment, a friend of mine came by and left a present. I was given four beautiful roses in a vase. I placed these roses behind my desk, a few steps removed from my consultation area. During our psychotherapy session, I happened to glance at the roses and felt that I would like to bring them nearer to us. I stood up, walked over to the desk, and brought the roses back to our consultation area. I gently placed them on the table near our chairs.

Elizabeth looked stunned. She asked me, "Why did you move those roses over here?" I answered, "I just felt that they were so beautiful that it might be nice to have them nearer to us." She replied, "Last night, I asked St. Thérèse, the Little Flower, to intercede before God on my behalf. I prayed that she would ask God to give me an extra measure of grace if I was indeed to go through this pain in psychotherapy. I asked for a sign that would confirm that I was to be in here with you. I also needed confirmation from God that you would hold on with me through therapy, no matter how trying it would become. I asked for this confirmation last night. I asked for roses. I am sure that God knows how much I enjoy the sight and smell of roses. I asked for the intercession of St. Thérèse, the Little Flower, just last night. Today, you stand up and bring roses over to the table next to us. So I know that I am doing what God has meant me to do."

Such a synchronous moment indeed attests to the fact that God is on our side. Being led by His Spirit, through inner promptings, always results in plentiful growth and change. Inward leading comes as a gentle but definite nudging. In quietness, the soul realizes God's inspiration to plumb the depths of the unconscious, of the spiritual world, of God Himself.

The Call

Fundamentally, the call of God, not individual desire, promotes spiritual growth. Certainly willful consent is necessary in the process of
spiritual and psychological growth. However, the object of desire
must be clear before the inner pull toward the object is felt. First God
calls, then the individual feels the desire to respond.

In writing about the lives of Jacob and Esau, St. Paul noted the
essential importance of recognizing the primacy of God's call, as he
wrote in his epistle to the Romans, " . . . though they were not yet
born and had done nothing good or bad, in order that God's purpose
of election might continue, not because of works but because of his
call, she was told, 'The elder will serve the younger' " (9:11, 12).
Once again, the call of God triggers the heart's latent desire to draw
close to Him.

St. Paul writes further, "So it depends not upon man's will or ex-
ertion, but upon God's mercy" (Rom. 9:16). No amount of effort can
conjure up the presence of God within the soul. God makes Himself
present willfully and mercifully to humankind. It is His utmost desire
to dwell in the hearts of men and women.

St. Paul quotes the prophet Isaiah, " 'Behold, I am laying in Zion
a stone that will make men stumble, a rock that will make them
fall; and he who believes in Him will not be put to shame' " (Rom.
9:33). God's call is constant in the heart of the believer. We have
only to listen in order to discern His words and direction for
our lives.

The telephone rang late one evening just before I retired. On the
other end was a very desperate and frightened voice. The young
woman said, "Dr. DeBlassie, I don't know what's happening, but everything around me feels evil." The moment she said that, I felt the
truthfulness of her words. Indeed a very cold and nefarious presence
seemed to be carried through the distance right into my study. I felt
what she felt. I knew that very dark emotions and a dark presence
tormented her.

I asked her, "What's been going on in your life lately?" She replied, "Every day and every night, all my husband and I can do is
fight. We fight over silly situations, meaningless problems, without
ever stopping. I can't take it anymore. Finally tonight, it seemed as
though he was ready to hit me. The children were screaming in the
back bedroom because of our fighting. Our rage toward each other

seemed so strong that I was frightened. All of a sudden, we both stopped fighting because we felt . . . sort of like evil all over. The room just seemed to turn cold. It felt like all of our rage brought the devil himself into our home. What should we do? We're afraid for both ourselves and our children. We've tried praying and telling the devil to leave. We tried calling our priest and he doesn't believe us. What can we do?"

I heard the cry of terror and desperation in her voice. I asked her to have her husband pick up the telephone extension so that the three of us could talk together. Having dealt with these situations before, I realized that dark feelings, left unresolved, can often lead into very disastrous circumstances. Indeed, the situation can become so dark that the demonic seems to take over. Deep-rooted evil necessitates both deep prayer and deep healing.

"What should I do?" she pleaded with me on the other end of the phone. Her husband also queried, "We'll do anything that we have to now. All this fighting just isn't worth it. I feel awful. We feel awful. The cold and evil feeling in our home is the worst feeling I've ever had. What can we do?"

I began by asking them to pray with me. The three of us together asked God's blessing on the moments to come. I then talked with them: "It's time to get to the bottom of this. Are you willing to try and listen to and understand each other?" With their affirmation, we proceeded.

Over the next thirty minutes, the three of us talked about their past hurts and pains. The anger and rage that they harbored toward each other came out. Neither of them wanted to continue hurting the other. Before this time, each one had been convinced of their position. No one had wanted to admit personal shortcomings. They had both been blaming each other. When blame takes the place of understanding, a demonic destructiveness results. For them, now, understanding superseded all desire to blame.

At the end of thirty minutes, she had forgiven him for his outbursts of rage and attack; he had forgiven her for her criticisms and haranguing. They forgave and understood each other. We all noticed that the presence of evil, which seemed so intense and invincible, was no longer felt. In its place were feelings of warmth and compassion. The sought-after deliverance from evil was accomplished through deep understanding and reconciliation. Forgiveness always causes the soul to find freedom.

This was a form of deep prayer. The initial prayer, together with the understanding and compassion exchanged by two hurting people, released the presence of God. Such contact with God is established when the human soul reaches out both to Him and to others. That is to say, when one's relationship with God is unimpeded and relationships with others are characterized by understanding and compassion, a divine presence can be experienced. Just as this husband and wife once felt the nearness of the demonic, they now knew the closeness and ever-caring presence of God.

Even though God greatly desires that you experience peace and harmony, unresolved feelings such as rage and fear need to be brought into His light for healing before peace of mind can be felt. In order to deal effectively with the demonic, the natural inroads that have left the person vulnerable must be dealt with. The healing of relationships goes hand in hand with deliverance from oppressive, negative forces.

Deep within each person resides feelings, thoughts, and intentions that are quite shadow-like and potentially destructive. It is these unconscious forces that erupt into everyday life, threatening relationships, life circumstances, and personal well-being. Darkness of this sort cripples the human heart if it is not brought into God's healing light.

The sacred scriptures state, " . . . for the Lord searches all hearts, and understands every plan and thought. If you seek Him, He will be found by you" (1 Chron. 28:9). Hidden motives and feelings interfere with union with God. Therefore, inner peace and harmony at times cannot be found. Tranquillity and serenity of mind depend upon a wholehearted relationship with God. If one is willing to acknowledge dark feelings such as deceit, anger, and unforgiveness, then the soul takes its first step toward increasing closeness with others and with God, thereby cultivating inner peace of mind.

With the revelation and working through of dark elements within the personality the presence of the Divine arises out of the depths of the individual. Each person innately contains a capacity to feel the presence of God. Once unconscious negative emotions and attitudes have been released and resolved, the felt presence of God, in depth, is readily available to the earnest seeker.

Thus, deep prayer means not only conversing with God within, but also means entering into understanding dialogue with another human being. Such conversation is indeed holy conversation when there is a

depth of exchange. The numinous, the holy, pervades every meaningful encounter between individuals.

My mentor and training analyst once told me that the deep presence of God could be found not only in times of formal prayer but
also during moments of compassionate understanding between people. Time spent giving your children undivided attention and listening are divine moments. During these times, you may, if you are
willing, open up your spiritual sensitivities and sense the presence of
God. Moments of extending yourself with listening and caring to your
spouse are moments of God's presence. If you will have eyes to see
and ears to hear, you will realize that God's call is a call that comes
during formal prayer, during the routine responsibilities of everyday
life, and during relaxed conversation characterized by attentiveness
and understanding.

God is truly a God who is bigger than your biggest problem. Allow
Him to be the big God for the big problems in your life by deepening
your life of prayer. Deep prayer unleashes deep power. Turning to God
in formal prayer and turning to God by exercising caring and compassion for others unleashes a divine energy that is far greater than any
malady or dilemma. God is a God just for you.

2

Inner Change Produces Outer Change

Let Go and Believe and Then You Will Receive

"Do not be conformed to this world but be transformed by the renewal of your mind . . . " (Rom. 12:2). Interior renewal or change precipitates external change. God always works from the inside out. With the life-changing experience of God in the soul as the result of deep prayer, a person begins to notice changes in external circumstances.

Not conforming any longer to the pattern of this world means to be no longer preoccupied, especially mentally or spiritually, by the endeavors of the world. "Do not love the world or the things in the world. If any one loves the world, love for the Father is not in him. For all that is in the world, the lust of the flesh and the lust of the eyes and the pride of life, is not of the Father but is of the world. And the world passes away, and the lust of it; but he who does the will of God abides for ever" (1 John 2:15–17). This scripture provides key characteristics of the pattern of the world.

First of all, the mental pattern of this world promotes cravings of a sinful nature. As the result of its fallen state, human nature may tend to focus on that which is negative and dark. For this reason many individuals continue in negative habits such as smoking, overeating, overdrinking and the like, even though they may realize that such habits promote ill health. These are the negative cravings of a fallen nature.

The lust of the eyes refers to coveting those objects that are not personally possessed. For instance, Jesus speaks of looking at a woman

24

lustfully being tantamount to committing adultery. Such lustful long-ing, be it for persons or things, detracts from spiritual well-being.

Lastly, the boasting of what one has and does also comes not from the Father but from the world. Boasting of social standing, material possessions, and professional or ecclesiastical standing are attitudes of the world. All of these things will eventually pass away. Prideful ar-rogance with regard to one's position in life burdens the soul and clutters the mind.

Interior detachment from externals promotes life with God. It leaves the soul unencumbered to experience the presence of God. In such a way, you are able to know Him in a deeper and deeper manner without being preoccupied by material concerns. It is not that you are uninvolved materially, for you have to live in the world. Rather, it is God who fills the mind as opposed to other thoughts, possessions, or activities.

This internal detachment from external encumbrances is not nec-essarily an easy matter. Our humanness naturally longs for many things. Some of these objects may even be of a "spiritual" nature.

One Sunday morning after Mass, my family and I decided to go out for breakfast. My wife Kathy and I found that our children were a particular delight that morning, so we decided to extend our outing. We visited an older part of our city that is filled with interesting little shops, many of them specializing in sacred art. Kathy and I especially enjoy sacred art.

As we walked into a little hidden-away shop, we both spotted a "santo." Santos are carved wooden figures made by craftsmen in northern New Mexico. A carved figure represents one of many saints. The santo is thought to have special meaning and inspiration. Kathy and I noticed a beautiful santo depicting Moses before the burning bush. The face of the santo was wrapped in ecstasy and the ardent love of God. We decided we had to have that santo.

The problem was that we "had to have" that santo. We both no-ticed that we really, really wanted to possess this piece of sacred art. In a sense, this material possession had taken possession of us. With this realization, we painfully decided not to make this purchase. We left the shop without the santo but perhaps a step closer to God.

For both Kathy and me, nothing means more than our relationship to God and the consequent fruit it bears in our relationship with each other. Once we understand that something has taken hold of our souls, something other than God, we attempt to rectify the situation immediately. We both experience a sense of peace in striving to leave all for His sake. We make an active effort to recognize those elements in our life that hold us back from Him. This is our first step in allowing inner change to take place in our hearts. Inevitably this produces a much more tranquil life for us.

Out of the depths of our personal prayer life, Kathy and I felt the strength to let go of that little santo which seemed so outwardly attractive. The pull to possess it was indeed very great. However, our love for God ran deeply enough to bypass this superficial and fleeting attraction.

Overcome Evil with Good

St. Paul articulates the primary characteristic of a deeply transformed mind when he writes, "Do not be overcome by evil, but overcome evil with good" (Rom. 12:21). This is to say that human nature may not only feel the attraction to materialism, but also to evil. By evil, we are referring to unconscious negative habits or behaviors that are chronically injurious to self or others.

When one has been assaulted by evil and attempts to return evil in kind, then one is made vulnerable to evil. Evil breeds evil, hate breeds hate. When hate is levied against you and you respond with hate, you will walk away from the situation more hate-filled than if you had responded with understanding. When you return hate for hate, hate is built up in your own soul, not released.

A young woman shared a very horrifying nightmare that was fraught with hate. In the nightmare, a terrifying-looking demon was attempting to kill her. When she fought back with this demon, cursing and swearing at him, the demon actually grew in size and power. She finally came to her senses in the dream and gently uttered the name Jesus, even though she was filled with fright. As she repeated the name "Jesus" over and over again, gently, very gently, the demon shrank, lessening in power moment by moment. Finally, the demon became smaller and smaller until it disappeared completely.

When I asked her about the meaning of this dream, she commented, "Whenever I notice imperfections in myself or others, I have a tendency to become enraged. I can hate myself and others who have faults. But this dream is telling me that such hate only worsens the problem and causes me to feel horrible. As I learn to understand myself and others more, and consequently grow closer to God, I actually feel better and better. The negative forces in my life then seem to lessen. I feel better on the inside as I am more loving and understanding with myself and with others."

For this young woman overcoming evil with good meant exercising understanding with regard to the weaknesses and limitations of herself and others. If she tore into herself with anger, this was a form of evil directed inwardly. It served merely to nourish the fault and intensify her self-destructive feelings. Only the goodness of understanding and the love of self and others settled her soul and helped her to grow. In this way, evil was overcome with good.

A Transformed Mind Clears the Way for the Divine

" . . . that you may prove what is the will of God, what is good and acceptable and perfect" (Rom. 12:2).

Once an individual begins the process of relinquishing external attachments and learning to overcome evil with good, the faculty of spiritual discernment is strengthened. In many cases, individuals notice that, without being bogged down by worldly preoccupations, their minds are more able to focus on God. Together with this, the sense of exercising compassion and understanding toward one's own faults as well as the failings of others helps to quiet the soul enough to hear the voice of God.

In other words, God's will becomes more and more discernible to the believer. A mind that is filled with anxious thoughts regarding ambitions and aspirations is a mind that suffers from confusion. In this state, a person can barely if at all notice God's presence. Oftentimes these individuals complain that they would do what God wanted them to do if only they knew what God wanted them to do. Unfortunately they are caught in a vicious cycle.

At one and the same time, they desire to know God's will but are confounding His quiet whisperings. They wonder if they should do this or that. The situation is considered from at least a dozen different perspectives without a clear decision ever being made. They are downtrodden by confusion.

A person of this sort is typically attempting to maintain a great deal of spiritual and emotional control. Even though the conscious desire seems to be to follow God, the unconscious pull is to remain in control of one's life. God's voice can be clearly heard only if one is willing to yield completely to Him. With such surrender, confusion gives way to clarity of mind. God's inner promptings and inspirations can then be quietly discerned.

A young woman who had recently suffered from a heart attack poured out her concerns to me: "I know I love my father, but whenever I'm around him, I can just feel my blood pressure rising. My ears seem to start ringing and they feel hot. They always do this when my blood pressure is rising.

"My father and I are actually very close. I call him every evening just to check on him. I really do want to talk with him, but it seems that every time we talk, he ends with a little dig. He was after me for years to finish my bachelor's degree. I finally did. At least a couple of times a week now, he ends our telephone conversation with the sense that he isn't quite pleased with me yet. He often says something to the effect, 'Well, maybe one day you'll be able to finish your master's degree. I know you could do it if you really wanted to. It would really make me happy.'

"This just causes me to feel awfully angry. Throughout my life, I have felt like I've never been able to please him. He did the same thing to me right before finishing my bachelor's degree. He egged me on and told me that he'd be happy if I just had my bachelor's degree. It just seems that he has never loved me for who I was. It was as though he was trying to live his life over again through me.

"He used to tell me, 'You need to have the courage to be all you want to be. Be the person you really are. But don't blame me if I don't like you for what you are.' So, I've been caught in the jam of trying to please him my entire life. For years and years I haven't known whether or not I was at fault. Maybe he was right. Maybe my feelings were wrong."

This patient expressed a deep level of confusion regarding her father. She didn't know whether her feelings with regard to him could be trusted. She felt that perhaps he was right. Maybe she was an underachiever. One thing she knew for sure: whenever she was around him, her blood pressure rose.

As a cardiac patient, it was very important for her blood pressure to remain controlled. She was having a very difficult time accomplishing this, even with the help of medication. She knew that the problem of her blood pressure was directly tied to her father and her feelings toward him.

A few weeks later she came up to me, after my presentation in a cardiac class, with a very peaceful and radiant smile. She reported, "About three nights after we talked, you told me about how you thought my high blood pressure was tied in to my anger toward my father. I really came to understand what you meant. I usually take about fifteen minutes to read my scripture before going to bed. During this time, I'm usually very relaxed. One night, when I had finished, your words came back to mind. In this relaxed state, feeling myself in the presence of God, I realized that my father would never accept me in the way that I wanted him to accept me. He would never fully understand me and I would never fully be able to satisfy him. I could literally destroy myself trying. At that moment, I saw him clearly and I realized that I needed to let him go. I finally understood my father. I was able to release him."

Remarkably enough, this young woman's blood pressure dramatically decreased. Her inner understanding and change of heart increased her physical health. After having struggled with her anger for years and years, she finally came to realize that it could destroy her. Depth of understanding, provided during a moment of consoling prayer, made God's will clear to her. She was to let go of her father, accept him for what he was, knowing that he would, in the foreseeable future, probably never change. In her words, "I felt God's inspiration in my heart that cleared my mind and helped me to see His will for me. He wanted me to let go and no longer expect my father to change one day. I feel free now. It's like my mind is brand new."

The Smaller We Are the More Room God Has

God's interior presence is greater or lesser, depending on one's degree of humility. Puffed up and inflated feelings regarding one's worth serve only to diminish the heartfelt presence of God. Contrary to this, a humble disposition in which the self is realistically appraised nourishes God's presence in the soul.

St. Paul writes, "For by the grace given to me I bid every one among you not think of himself more highly than he ought to think, but to think with sober judgment, each according to the measure of faith which God has assigned him" (Rom. 12:3). Out of his own life experience St. Paul realized the importance of humility. In fact, a truly transformed, enlightened, genuine follower of Jesus can be noticed by the quality of humility that emanates from within.

C. G. Jung commented on the reality and importance of such humility,

> . . . even the enlightened person remains what he is, and is never more than his own limited ego before the One who dwells within him, whose form has no knowable boundaries, Who encompasses him on all sides, fathomless as the abysms of the earth and vast as the sky.

As the light of God floods the soul, humility always embraces the person. Thus, a true encounter with God can be judged according to the degree of humbleness that follows. True conversion helps an individual truly to know both limitations and strengths, failings and achievements, and most of all the full nature of the human condition. In fact, the closer one is to God, the more human and real he or she is. Cardinal Newman noted,

> Do you desire to be great? Make yourself little. There is a mysterious connection between real advancement and self-effacement. If you minister to the humble and the despised, if you feed the hungry, tend the sick, succor the distressed; if you bear with the forward, submit to insult, endure ingratitude, render good for evil, you are, as by divine charm, getting power over the world and rising among the creatures. God has established this law. Thus He does His wonderful works. His instruments are poor and despised; the world hardly knows their names, or not at all. They are busied about what the world thinks to be petty actions, and no one minds them. They are apparently set on no great works; nothing is seen to come of what they do; they seem to fail. Nay, even as regards religious objects which they themselves profess to desire, there is no natural and visible connection between their doings and sufferings and these desirable ends; but there's an unseen connection in the kingdom of God. They rise by falling. Plainly so, for no condescension can be so great as that of our Lord himself. Now the more they abase themselves, the more like they are to Him, the greater must be their power with Him. . . . When a man discerns in himself the most sin and humbles himself most, when his comeliness seems to him to vanish away and all his graces to wither, when he feels disgusted himself, and revolts at the thought of himself—seems to himself all dust and ashes, all foulness and odiousness, then it is that he is really rising in the kingdom of God.

After all of this talk of self-effacement, it is interesting to note that St. Paul begins his message on humility by referring to the grace that has been given to him: "For by the grace given to me . . ." (Rom. 12:3). He seems to refer to this grace as the source and confirmation of his authority to teach the Roman church. In other words, God's grace empowered him as an individual, imbued him with self-worth, and authorized him to teach what he knew about the life of the soul.

Authentic humility actually increases one's sense of healthy self-worth. Confidence and a surety with regard to one's abilities are part of humility. Neither overestimation nor underestimation of capacities and abilities are apparent in the truly humble soul. Rather, a realistic sense of self-worth and value accompany spiritual meekness.

St. Paul must have felt the divine assurance of God's love for him whenever he recalled that moment of grace in which he met the Master on the road to Damascus. God literally opened up the heavens for Saul of Tarsus. God went out of His way for Saul. Grace was directed from heaven to earth and into the heart of Saul of Tarsus by the hand of Him who loved Saul with an everlasting love.

St. Paul described another moment of very personal grace when he wrote, "I know a man in Christ who fourteen years ago was caught up to the third heaven—whether in the body or out of the body I do not know, God knows. And I know that this man was caught up into Paradise . . . he heard things that cannot be told which man may not utter" (2 Cor. 12:2–4).

It is these moments of grace, these special touches from God, that Paul must have been remembering as he wrote to the Roman church and referred to the grace that had been given to him. Before he taught the church about humility, he emphasized the grace of God. This grace imparts self-worth and value to all who receive it. God's love for you is so deep that he will open the heavens to touch you in the depths of your heart if you will receive Him.

This sort of grace is not some sort of angelic fairy dust sprinkled from heaven to earth and into your soul. True grace is God living deep in you. God's love and nature are of incredible quality. His character lives in you. His excellence and goodness are in you. You are a person of great value and importance in God's eyes.

One evening after I had finished a retreat for a local parish a woman in her early sixties approached me. She exclaimed, "Dr. De-Blassie, I just have to tell you that I finally realized how much God loves me. For forty years I have been allowing my husband to call me every name in the book and treat me any way he wanted to. I thought this was the Christian thing to do. He would make any sort of demand on me that he wanted, and I would think that I had to fulfill it.

"I read the book *Women Who Love Too Much*. That book helped me to realize that I had been an abused woman for many years. Although my husband has struck me only six or seven times during the course of our marriage, he had verbally abused me almost daily. I thought that it was Christian virtue and humility to put up with this. I now see that I am a child of God and have worth as a person.

"One day I finally told him, 'I don't deserve to be treated this way. And I won't put up with it anymore. I want you in counseling, or else we may have to separate. I love you and I don't want to be without you, but I won't put up with the abuse.' "

She noted that his mouth fell wide open with surprise and disbelief that she had spoken to him in this way. "Actually," she said, "I shocked myself, I had never spoken up for myself before. Finally I realized that God did not expect me to be abused. It has been a couple of months now since we both entered into counseling. I can tell that we're making progress, but at the same time I know that we have a long way to go. It took this way of shocking him, threatening him with separation, before our relationship could change. I know now that God loves me. I am a person of worth."

A healthy self-esteem, such as this woman was beginning to experience, is indicative of real emotional and spiritual health. It affirms all that is of value, all that is good, and all that is meaningful in a human life. Confidence, courage, and if you would, a healthy pride epitomize the truly humble person.

I think of Moses. He was called by God to effect powerfully the course of salvation history. In the natural realm of development he had a very low sense of self-esteem. He stuttered and seemed afraid to exercise leadership. Rather than leading God's people out of bondage, he would have been more content to care for his father-in-law's sheep for the rest of his life.

After God appeared to him in the burning bush he acquired a new sense of self-confidence. This moment of grace enabled him to approach Pharaoh and command that God's people be set free. This dramatic encounter between good and evil tested all of Moses' internal resources. Once again, in the natural sense, he was a very inferior sort of person. Once touched by the grace of God he became empowered with strength and courage. He felt the infusion of grace, the infilling of God living deep in him. He now had the spiritual vigor and tenacity to meet the most demanding of life's challenges.

Now that we have somewhat understood that a good self-image is an integral part of a Christian life we must take the next step to realize fully that humility goes hand in hand with self-esteem. An individual's ability to appraise correctly his or her own strengths and weaknesses permits maximum availability to God. One does not attempt to engage in activities outside that realm of ability or calling. For this reason, St. Paul writes, "I bid every one among you not to think of himself more highly than he ought to think, but to think with sober judgment, each according to the measure of faith God has assigned him" (Rom. 12:3).

Oftentimes an individual who exerts himself or herself outside of their genuine gifts is operating from a position of egocentricity. Personal needs for acclamation and adulation become quite obvious. Frequently, abuses of power and control run rampant. This typically produces fruits of dissension and divisiveness.

This is not to say that a truly humble person is nonaggressive. In fact, an individual who pretends to be humble via the rejection of all aggression is in a state of arrested psychological development. Such a position denies the validity of aggression as one of the basic and natural components of the human psyche. This is actually quite a dangerous predicament.

Once human aggression is denied on a conscious level it breeds an unconscious sort of violence. Hatred and rage are then inflicted on others in a very passive and subtle manner. A supposedly nonaggressive person may, in fact, be one who suppresses his or her aggression and lives in a simulation of peace. Such a one cannot quite understand why others find him or her so difficult to relate to and so frustrating. In essence, destruction is spread unconsciously into relationships.

True humility permits one to take a stand for all that is meaningful and of value in life. The pride of the ego, power, and greed give way to a willingness and a courage to suffer self-sacrifice. In the end, if one is to be true to his or her humanity, aggression must be accepted and integrated. Jesus recognized this as he said of Himself, "Do not think that I have come to bring peace on earth; I have not come to bring peace, but a sword" (Matt. 10:34).

There does come a time, however, in spiritual development when one has no more need to fight. Herein an individual has sufficiently integrated instinctual aggression so that it is no longer denied or inflicted in a harmful manner. Life is lived without inflicting hurt of any kind. Owing to repeated self-sacrifice the believer enters into a state that is beyond the opposites of love and hate. He or she accepts participation in the suffering of all humanity. This increases one's ability to understand others in a compassionate and empathic manner.

Thus, we must learn to fight for that which is of great value and meaning. This insures the growth of personality and also solidifies spiritual development. Finally, however, one eventually becomes confident enough in personal strength so that fighting can be laid down and fullness of humility assumed. In this, the words of St. John the Baptist ring true: "He must increase, but I must decrease" (John 3:30).

The Antidote to Spiritual and Psychological Harm

Spiritual harm is suffered whenever the soul is divorced from interior realities. In our modern-day age, the emphasis is on materialism and the external world. The empirical model which bases everything on experimental evidence is the mainstay of everyday life. Decisions are made based on facts rather than faith.

This is not meant to demean experimental science. Rather, when this is the only basis for an individual's existence, spiritual sterility and harm are encountered. Empirical facts help us to develop and perceive technologically. However, a purely technological approach to life mechanizes human nature and even relationships. Without a heartfelt knowledge of God, neurosis and a meaningless existence eventually result.

The psychological implications of this are manifold. Neuroses of various sorts emerge when the individual feels spiritually alienated. Symptoms ranging from depression, anxiety, and various stress-related disorders to blatant psychotic states can be perpetrated through spiritual meaninglessness. One emotional problem after another is the lot of those separated from true spirituality.

A genuine encounter with the holiness of God fills up one's spiritual void and enhances psychological health. Men and women are created whole. With depth of spirituality comes depth of psychological wholeness. By working through various psychological conflicts the individual is more predisposed to enter into a living relationship with God.

The reason for this interplay between the spiritual and the psychological comes down to one issue: love. As St. Paul notes in his letter to the Romans, "Love does no wrong to a neighbor; therefore love is the fulfilling of the law" (13:10). Love is the force that radiates throughout sound Christian spirituality and psychology.

In depth psychology it is well accepted that emotional suffering can result from a lack of love. With an abundance of love during the childhood years a person grows into adulthood feeling secure, confident, and healthy. If childhood is troubled by constant relationships with angry and abusing people the adult years are filled with insecurity and torment.

Matters of spirituality are profoundly affected by psychological development. If other people are viewed as threatening and harmful, God will also be seen as similarly hostile. If one perceives people as nurturing and understanding, God will also be regarded as a benevolent person.

Positive experiences during the early years thus create the readiness for a healthy spirituality. Otherwise, a relationship with God may be resisted as are relationships with people. Through depth psychotherapy a hurting person may be brought to a point of resolving past pain. Such a person is then open to internalizing love from other people and God. A relationship with God also promotes psychological health. That is to say, even though an individual has been greatly wounded by other people, once she or he experiences the loving kindness of God the Father, these afflictions are soothed little by little. Psychological and spiritual growth thus complement each other, since both are based in love.

The major problem for modern-day humankind, then, is one of psychological and spiritual crisis. Carl Jung confirms that for our modern Western world the trauma of the human soul rings out loud and clear:

> The gigantic catastrophes that threaten us today are not elemental happenings of a physical or biological order, but psychic events. To a quite terrifying degree, we are threatened by wars and revolutions which are nothing other than psychic epidemics. . . . instead of being at the mercy

of wild beasts, earthquakes, landslides, and inundations, modern man is
battered by the elemental forces of his own psyche.

The antidote, therefore, to such a human peril lies in encountering
the God of love directly and in and through human relationships.
The God of the universe who deeply loves you desires to heal all of
your psychological torment. He yearns to recreate your body, mind,
and spirit. He will impart new life to you as you earnestly seek Him.

Inner and Outer Harmony

Harmony with God produces harmony with the environment. When
things are moving along in an in-depth and peaceful manner in one's
relationship with God, this will be reflected in the external world.
As the soul is in a healthy state, so external relationships and activities also are very constructive and creative. In this spiritual state
right things happen around us instead of wrong things.

With ill temper and disagreeable moods come disintegrating problems. When one is chronically upset and angry everything seems to
go wrong. Rather than working with you it is as if life is opposing
you. The more disintegrated a person feels inside the more disintegrated and out-of-sorts their life appears to be.

Projected psychological disorder characterizes black magic and
witchcraft. Witches and magicians project their inner chaos into people or situations. This, in effect, disintegrates and destroys whatever
or whoever is affected. It is a very definite and disorderly power.

Contrary to this, the power of prayer stems from spiritual harmony
and order. The great Christian mystics permitted themselves to attain
deep union with God. Such interior harmony required a death to
their egocentricities and selfish disorders. The result was miraculous.

St. Gertrude, a Benedictine abbess, for example, was acclaimed to
be able to influence the weather. Stories abounded with regard to her
ability to save a harvest from a storm, bring about the cessation of a
severe frost, and stop hail by prayer. In her documented prayers, she
noted that she never attempted to impose her egocentric desire on
God, but merely desired to draw His attention to the facts. She focused on achieving complete harmony between herself and God, a
harmony which caused the miraculous to occur.

The outer effect of deep harmony with God is beautifully conveyed in the following widely told story:

There was a terrible drought in that part of China where a young scholar was living. After all the ways to bring rain that the people knew had been tried, they decided to send for a rainmaker. This interested the young scholar very much, and he was careful to be there when the rain-maker arrived. The man came in a covered cart, a small wizened old man who sniffed the air with evident distaste as he got out of the cart, and asked to be left alone in a small cottage outside the village; even his meals were to be laid down outside the door.

Nothing was heard from him for three days, then it not only rained, but there was also a big downfall of snow, unknown at that time of the year. Very much impressed, the young scholar sought the rainmaker out and asked him how it was that he could make rain, and even snow. The rainmaker replied, "I have not made the snow; I am not responsible for it." The young scholar insisted that there was a terrible drought until he came, and then after three days they even had quantities of snow. The old man answered, "Oh, I can explain that. You see, I come from a place where the people are in order; they are in harmony with God; so the weather is also in order. But, directly I got here, I saw the people were out of order and they also infected me. So I remained alone until I was once more deeply in harmony in God. And then, of course, it rained and snowed."

Jim, a young minister, had been suffering through severe marital conflict for eight years. Each evening his wife would complain, "You always have time for other people. You never have time for me and your children. Why don't you start practicing what you preach?"

In actuality, Jim was a very sensitive and giving husband and fa-ther. His wife Jane, on the other hand, was very irritable and easily provoked. She suffered from chronic gynecological problems. This precipitated a great deal of moodiness and bickering on her part. Jim was concerned that he was unable to find a way to satisfy his wife.

After much prayer, he felt an interior assurance that all would be well as long as he would continue trusting God in the matter. One evening his wife began her nagging in the usual fashion. He finally spoke up and said, "I've had it. I have been very understanding and compassionate with you. For all these years you've been nagging at me. We have to get to the bottom of this. You have a problem and it's not me."

Jim recalled that at the very moment of exercising firm love with his wife, a very deep and impressive thought came to his mind. He sensed an interior discernment that his wife had undergone a sexual problem before their marriage. This left her with such guilt that pain ran rampant in the parts of her body associated with the incident. He told her, "I don't know what happened before we got married. But I have a strong feeling that something very awful happened to you. I feel that I'm paying the price for that now."

Needless to say, Jane was stunned. She thought that this secret had been tucked away in her heart. No one else knew about it. Somehow, in some way, Jim had come to find out about it. She cried and talked and talked. For the next four hours they talked and prayed together. This provided just the opening Jane needed to begin working through this long-held horror. Jim's firm love and God-given inspiration saw her through to the resolution and healing she so badly needed.

Jim noted that this sudden intuitive realization was directly linked to the many hours of prayer he had spent regarding the matter. He made the conscious decision to approach God daily for an answer. With such diligence the answer came out of the depths of his unconscious. From out of his soul sprang the intuitive discernment about what troubled his wife. This is the fruit of persistent love and deep prayer.

Standing on the Edge of a Miracle

Sustained deep prayer frequently ushers in God's miraculous intervention. God is ready and willing to meet our every need. In fact, He may be ready and quite available to minister to us in a rather unexpected manner. Miraculous happenings are quite within God's ability. The story of Joshua and the battle of Jericho is a case in point. After the death of Moses, Joshua assumed command. The Lord spoke to him saying, " . . . as I was with Moses, so I will be with you; I will not fail you or forsake you" (Josh. 1:5).

This new responsibility required great single-heartedness of devotion to God on the part of Joshua. He was responsible for the physical and spiritual welfare of the entire Israelite nation, numbering perhaps one million people. Such unwavering commitment to serve God empowered Joshua to both hear the voice of God and to lead the people forth into God's blessing:

The Israelites were united in following Joshua: And they answered Joshua, "All that you have commanded us we will do, and wherever you send us we will go. Just as we obeyed Moses in all things, so we will obey you; only may the Lord your God be with you, as he was with Moses! Whoever rebels against your commandment and disobeys your words, whatever you command him, shall be put to death. Only be strong and of good courage." (Josh. 1:16–18)

Unity prepared God's chosen people inwardly and outwardly to inherit His blessings. This has great pertinence to matters of the soul. The heart that is divided with regard to the spiritual life is not only vulnerable but quite weak. Weakness of this sort stems from a lack of wholeheartedly yielding oneself to God. God can empower the soul only to the degree of personal availability to Him. Partial availability renders partial strength. Total yieldedness causes a saturation of the soul with divine empowering.

Having listened intently to God and having heard His word, Joshua told the people, " 'Sanctify yourselves; for tomorrow the Lord will do wonders among you" (Josh. 3:5). Before entering the land of Jericho the Israelites needed to cross the River Jordan. Joshua commanded His people to travel to the Jordan with the priest carrying the Ark of the Covenant ahead of the group. He then told the priests to touch their feet to the water; God would take care of the rest. The priests proceeded to march on, carrying the Ark of the Covenant on their shoulders. They walked up to the River Jordan. When they reached the river they did not stop but proceeded to continue on their way. With each step the water parted in front of them " . . . and rose up in a heap far off." (Josh. 3:16).

The miraculous occurred as faith was exerted. When all of one's resources have seemingly been spent, when one's back is against the wall, when it seems like there is no way out, this is the time God can come through. At these moments the defenses of the ego have been weakened. One is open and vulnerable in a very healthy and creative manner. The soul is yielded fully to God. The miraculous is ready to happen.

Right at the moment of your most intense pain you are standing at the edge of a miracle. At the sight of the entire Israelite army crossing the River Jordan the army of Jericho fled in terror. Jericho made preparations for the Israelites to launch a full-scale attack. Little did they know that Joshua had a different plan in mind.

Rather than immediately rushing into battle Joshua called the people into prayer. For the first time in thirty-nine years the feast of Passover was celebrated. Spiritual worship of this sort nourished their souls for what was about to transpire. Before God required more faith to be exerted in the external world, He made sure that his people were spiritually fed.

Once one feels the impulse to engage in some activity for the sake of Christ, spiritual preparations must be made. Substantive outer activity must issue forth from an inner life force. Deep prayer nourishes the soul with the creativity and life-giving forcefulness that is required for building and developing in the external world.

After celebrating the Passover Joshua once again withdrew into deep prayer. An angel appeared before him. Joshua at first did not know who this being was. He asked:

> "Are you for us, or for our adversaries?" And he said, "No; but as commander of the army of the Lord I have now come." And Joshua fell on his face to the earth, and worshiped, and said to him, "What does my lord bid his servant?" And the commander of the Lord's army said to Joshua, "Put off your shoes from your feet; for the place where you stand is holy." And Joshua did so. (Josh. 5:13–15)

Here Joshua encountered the *numinosum*—the holy. The very holiness of God overcame him. Even the ground on which he stood was saturated with God's holiness. This mystical touch opened Joshua's mind and heart to understand what he was about to do. The *numinosum* floods the heart with God. It is meant to signal the dawn of a new level of development for the soul. It marks new growth. With it, the individual has the power to live more deeply in God and more creatively in the external world.

John, a very devout Catholic, explained to me his experience of God speaking to him during a very brief moment of deep prayer. He recalled, "This was at a time when I needed to hear God's voice inside me. Sometimes when he speaks to me it doesn't take any more than a moment or so. I needed to make a decision regarding a business matter. I needed God's help.

"I closed the doors to my office. I became very, very quiet as I sat behind my desk. I descended deep into my soul. It's there that God speaks to me. I never hear him in an audible voice. When he speaks I can tell because of a very clear-minded sense of inspiration that I receive.

"After two or three minutes of being very silent and very deep I sensed God's presence and I heard Him speak. The inspiration came through loud and clear from within me. I was not to move ahead with this particular business transaction. I felt God guiding me on this everyday matter of business. I knew it was God speaking to me because I felt Him. When I received this inspiration my mind was clear and immediately my heart was at peace. I felt no more confusion or restlessness. When it is His voice speaking to me I feel tranquil and filled with a very natural sense of solid faith."

God's revelation to the human soul transpires during the heart-to-heart relationship with Him that takes place during deep prayer. Nothing else preoccupies the mind save God during these divine moments. One is literally consumed with an awareness of His presence. God is all in all. All things become strikingly clear. One looks into matters with spiritual eyes discerning what is right and wrong, sifting through to God's will from natural will.

Just as God spoke to Joshua He longs to speak with you today. Quiet yourself. Listen. He is ready to speak to you. You will sense an impression that will leave you feeling encouraged, edified, faith-filled, and very much at peace. This is the voice of God. This is God speaking to you.

As Joshua listened intently to God speaking to him, he received guidance:

And the Lord said to Joshua, "See, I have given into your hand Jericho, with its king and mighty men of valor. You shall march around the city, all the men of war going around the city once. Thus shall you do for six days. And seven priests shall bear seven trumpets of rams' horns before the ark; and on the seventh day you shall march around the city seven times, the priests blowing the trumpets. And when they make a long blast with the ram's horn, as soon as you hear the sound of the trumpet, then all the people shall shout with a great shout; and the wall of the city will fall down flat, and the people shall go up every man straight before him." (Josh. 6:2–5)

The common-sense approach would have been to attack the problem directly. Joshua and his military men would have immediately pounced on the city of Jericho. This was man's way. This was not God's way.

Frequently it seems as though God has a more roundabout way of accomplishing things than we do. He seems to be very deliberate and patient. At times it seems as though it takes a thousand years for God to listen to heartfelt prayers. He does have a purpose in this. Such patient waiting requires the soul to remain humble before Him, realizing that it is only through His power that a solution will come. This humility saves one from inflation and pride. The more one is dependent upon God, the less one is dependent on ego.

As the king of Jericho looked down on the Israelites from atop his city walls he noticed them marching around the city walls. Each day for six days they would march around once. Once and only once each day they would march.

I could imagine God's purpose in doing this. It left the Jericho army completely befuddled. It was a form of mental warfare. After six days of being very uptight, not knowing when the Israelites would attack, the army of Jericho must have been very much at wits' ends. In a sense, God did not allow the Israelites to take external action with regard to this problem before He had worked on the difficulty from the inside Himself. He wanted to wear away the problem from the inside out.

The miraculous was ready to occur. In God's way and in God's timing, the Israelites' big problem would be overcome. Not in their way, but in God's way victory ensued.

Finally on the seventh day, the Israelites marched around Jericho not one time but seven times. The people then stopped and shouted a mighty shout of praise to God. All mental and spiritual energy was focused on God, not on the problem. The walls of Jericho came tumbling down.

When you have done all that you can possibly do with regard to your problem be assured that you are standing on the edge of a miracle. Continue listening to God. Allow Him to speak with quiet and steady inspiration in your soul.

He will always guide you with words of encouragement. You will sense an inner assurance that He will come through for you as you wait patiently for Him. You will feel a sense of humility knowing that it is God who is at work. He begins by working on the unseen dimensions of the problem. This is why you do not notice results right away. Soon, as you are faithful to Him, the outer results will be manifest. Because of your faithfulness you will come to understand that all along you have been standing on the edge of a miracle.

Invisible Faith—Invisible Fear

The story is told of a young woman and a snake. One afternoon a young woman received a knock at her door. She opened the door just barely an inch to peek outside. When she saw the snake she quickly slammed the door.

The snake spoke up loudly, "Please listen to me. I'm a tired-out and very weary snake. I need somewhere to rest for a while. Please listen to me."

Once again the young woman opened the door just an inch. She replied to the snake, "You might be tired and need rest, but you are a snake. You are a man-eating snake. And I would never let you in my home."

The snake answered, "Please understand me, I am so tired and worn out. I wouldn't hurt anyone. I couldn't hurt anyone. I'm just too tired. Please just let me rest a while in your home. Please. You wouldn't turn away such a pitiful fellow, would you?"

As the story goes, the young woman finally felt sorry for the snake. She decided that he was so worn out and drained that she couldn't possibly turn him away. She allowed him in her home. The moment she let him in the snake pounced on her and proceeded to devour her. She screamed out wildly to the snake, "But you said you wouldn't hurt me." Cunningly, the snake remarked, "But you knew I was a snake when you let me into your home."

Those forces that threaten spiritual well-being are often, like the snake, not readily apparent. They are deceiving and invisible. The deadliest and most invisible culprit of all is fear.

Fear devours the soul in a moment's time. It leaves one depleted and despairing. When one gives way under the weight of a depressive mood, engendered by doubt and insecurity, the soul is crippled. Invisible, inner doubt produces horrible suffering. It causes one to doubt the reality of God's life-giving power. God may come through for others; but in a state like this, one questions whether God can be personally depended upon. Psychological suffering runs rampant.

At this point an individual has a choice. Lying down under the weight of this doubt-infested mood will generate incredible and meaningless suffering. Self-pity and an egocentered preoccupation possess the soul. Nothing is learned and therefore nothing is gained. Suffering of this sort is empty and without purpose.

Rather than choosing this emptiness an individual may exercise his or her will to feel and face their doubt and fear. Intense personal doubt can feel terrifying. It can leave one racked with horror. The fright is one of being totally abandoned by the love and support of others and the providence of God.

The soul endures this suffering knowing that there is something to learn. For the Christian there is always hope. Jesus' life did not end with death. He rose from the dead. Light will come at the end of life's dark tunnels. However, the tunnels must be crawled through before reaching the light.

When fear is contained, suffered through, and understood, the individual experiences increased personal growth and awareness of God's presence. For this reason alone such pain is tolerable, although perhaps barely so. The one who undergoes this type of meaningful suffering grows with great freedom toward greater knowledge of self and of the risen Jesus.

When one refuses to accept the pain of everyday life, suffering becomes possessive. The more you run away from the pain and suffering in your life the more powerful it becomes. On the other hand, conscious suffering does not crush the soul. In fact, as such pain is willingly accepted it becomes lighter and lighter. In the words of Jesus, "My yoke is easy, and my burden is light" (Matt. 11:30).

This being the case, invisible fears and doubts can be said to signal the potential for increased growth and development. Kept in darkness, they fester and immobilize the soul. As you bring your fears and doubts before God daily, willing to suffer whatever this cross brings, self-knowledge increases and your relationship with God deepens. Only in the light of His presence does the pain of invisible doubt and fear gradually ease.

Once again, as we look into the life of that great prophet of old, Joshua, we find an exemplar of faith. After the tremendous victory of Jericho one might think that Joshua could take it easy for a while. This was hardly the case. Joshua's greatest test of faith came not from Jericho but from the battle of Ai.

After having conquered Jericho the Lord commanded Joshua to take possession of the land of Ai. Ai was a very small country with only a tiny army compared to the military force of Israel. However, this tiny land posed big problems for Joshua.

Three thousand Israelite soldiers advanced to capture the land of Ai. Without a moment's notice a band of soldiers from Ai descended upon Israel and killed thirty-six men. This terrified Joshua's militia. The scriptures note, "And the hearts of the people melted, and became as water" (Josh. 7:5).

Joshua ardently petitioned God concerning this matter. He said:

" . . . Alas O Lord God, why hast thou brought this people over the Jordan at all, to give us into the hands of the Amorites, to destroy us? Would that we had been content to dwell beyond the Jordan! O Lord, what can I say, when Israel has turned their backs before their enemies! For the Canaanites and all the inhabitants of the land will hear of it, and will surround us, and cut off our name from the earth. . . . (Josh. 7:7–9)

[The Lord then answered Joshua,] " . . . the people of Israel cannot stand before their enemies; they turn their backs before their enemies, because they have become a thing for destruction. I will be with you no more, unless you destroy the devoted things from among you" (Josh. 7:12–13)

Doubt had crept into Israel. God had given explicit instructions that all of the silver, gold, bronze, and iron from Jericho was to be placed into the treasury of the Lord's house. One man out of Israel, Achan, doubted God's provision for his life. He secretly kept a beautiful robe, some silver, and some gold. He hid these treasures in a hole dug inside his tent. Rather than trusting God to provide for him, Achan took the matter into his own hands. He doubted God's provision for his life and sought his security in mammon.

Achan's doubt left Israel vulnerable to its enemies. Once his sin was exposed, Achan and his entire family, together with all that they owned, were stoned and burned. Needless to say, God was very firm and direct in dealing with faithlessness.

Since the soul was made for God and God for the soul, we can surmise that our souls likewise do not tolerate faithlessness. Complete dependence and reliance upon God nourishes the life of the soul. Giving way to doubts and discouraging moods plunders from the soul riches and treasures. Indeed, one can find the pearl of great price only after having endured intensive testings of faith. Self-destruction results from a faithless approach to life. The soul develops and grows with the cultivation of deep and single-hearted faith in God.

In the process of maturing, the development of single-heartedness becomes an ongoing challenge. All of us continually experience greater or lesser doubts. This fact does not detract from spiritual intensity. What matters is the manner in which temptations toward faithlessness are handled.

Joshua immediately admitted his weak faith. He prayed until late evening, telling God about his worries and concerns. In other words, he immediately admitted the dark emotions within him. He ushered them into the light of God's presence. Here he found consolation and resolution.

Unlike Joshua, Achan suppressed his inner doubts. This was symbolized by the burying of the stolen treasure from Jericho. Achan maintained his entrenchment in egocentricity and self-reliance. In the end, he was destroyed by his own suppressed inner misgivings and insecurities.

Joshua's abandonment before God and earnest prayer represent the struggle of the soul to make conscious before God undesirable elements of the personality. This requires painful self-awareness. Many people adamantly avoid any type of self-awareness for fear of intruding on their superficial sense of well-being.

In deep prayer the presence of God illumines the soul, baring the hidden motives of the heart. Feelings of shame, guilt, fear, and negativism are aroused. With intensely honest self-examination God is free to heal the soul. Self-reflection evokes the humility necessary to invite the presence of God. In and through humble soul-searching, always seeking the healing light of Christ, the personality is gradually made whole.

I remember a dream of mine depicting a terrible battle with personal fear. At this time in my life I had been struggling with doubts concerning matters of great personal importance. Circumstances seemed at odds with my objectives. Nothing was coming together. Waves of fear began to dampen my spirits.

In this dream, I was in a room approximately ten feet by ten feet in size. It was gray, dingy, and stark. Out of the only window, a very small window, I noticed two Nazi guards approaching me. They forcefully entered the room.

As I backed away from them, they confronted me hostilely. The one in charge said, "You must denounce Jesus Christ or you will die. If you are willing to tell us right now that you are no longer a Christian we will allow you to live. If you continue believing in Jesus we will kill you. We will close the doors to this room and poisonous gas fumes will be yours to breathe. You will die."

This dream was so real that I told myself in the dream, "This can't be real. This can't be happening to me. Surely I must be dreaming." The dream was reality for me.

All sorts of thoughts flashed through my mind. I remembered the Christian martyrs of old. Could I die for Him? Momentarily, fear swept through me. From the top of my head to the soles of my feet I trembled. What would I do?

As I reflected on all of this, an inspiration came. I realized that at the moment of facing death Christian martyrs all experienced a very singular grace of holiness and faith. This anointing transported them from this world to the next spiritually, so that their physical dilemma was of little consequence to them. In that next second I knew that His grace would be sufficient for me.

I looked at the two Nazi guards and asserted, "Jesus is my Lord now and for eternity. I will be with Him now and I will be with Him forever." My being cried forth this proclamation of faith.

The commander shouted, "Then you will die!" The guards reached over to shove me to the floor. Before they reached me I dropped to the floor so that I would willingly give myself over to death for Him. No one could force or push me into this sacrifice. With faith I fell to the floor.

I heard the door slam as I lay on the floor, my face pressing against the cold concrete. I uttered, "Lord Jesus." A holy faith came over me. I will never forget the awesome presence of God within and about me. Nothing mattered save Him. In Him I lived and moved and had my being. I knew that I was His in life and in death. I knew the loving embrace of Him who down through the ages had enveloped with solace and comfort those dying for the faith.

I heard the hissing sound of gas leaking into the room. As I breathed these vapors my consciousness faded and I felt only the presence of God. I knew I had been faithful and had not given in to invisible fear. Everything around me grew dim.

As I breathed my last breath of air (at least it seemed this way) I heard the hissing stop. The door opened. I vaguely saw four or five very close friends rush into the cell. One of them picked me up and quickly carried me out.

As he held me in his arms he said, "You have been faithful to Him. He knows of your faithfulness. You are very near to Him." The dream ended and I awoke.

I gazed around my bedroom and felt disoriented. I could not believe that this had been a dream. I was there. I knew I was there. I
suddenly became aware of the presence of holiness in and about me.
The same presence of God that filled my soul in the dream now
blessed me in my waking state.

Upon reflection I realized that I had fought the battle of faith in
my soul and emerged victoriously. His grace had seen me through.
From within I sensed a new, authentic, and invigorating faith.

In a very synchronistic manner the outside circumstances that
troubled me began to be resolved. A coming together of events very
solidly and cohesively took place. My problem had been solved by
confronting the invisible fear that threatened me interiorly. With the
battle waged and won in the soul God's grace was freed to transform
outer circumstances.

The Christian need not be disabled by invisible fear. God's grace
will meet each man and woman at the point of his or her deepest
need. When the soul feels terrifying fear, it can rest assured that
abundant grace lies close at hand. For those living in the light of
Christ, invisible faith always overcomes invisible fear.

Deep Inner Exploration

The healing light of Jesus Christ emanates from the depths of the
soul. The mystery of Christ Jesus can be understood only by careful
and sensitive exploration into His presence within. His voice, the
word of God, is discerned only by those with ears to hear and open
hearts to receive. He is available to all who choose to seek Him
deeply from their heart.

St. Paul witnessed,

> I became a minister according to the divine office which was given to
> me for you, to make the word of God fully known, the mystery hidden
> for ages and generations but now made manifest to his saints. To them
> God chose to make known how great among the Gentiles are the riches
> of the glory of this mystery, which is Christ in you, the hope of glory.
> (Col. 1:25–27)

Explorations into the deeper regions of the soul uncover the presence of Christ Jesus. This is a mysterious experience indeed. One

must look intently within before it can be discovered. At one and the same time Christ Jesus is very available and yet very mysterious. He is there for you the moment you call upon His name, yet it is only when you seek Him with your whole heart that you will find Him.

Upon awakening the presence of Jesus within you, a startling discovery can be made. The holiness from His presence fills you through and through. Although you may have been frightened, indeed terrified to abandon yourself completely to Him, once you have done so an awesome holiness and comfort fills your being. Holiness of this magnitude creates new life and well-being.

C. G. Jung frequently told the story about Brother Klaus. This man was a very devout Swiss monk who lived near Zurich. His great spirituality and holiness were known far and wide. In fact, he was venerated throughout his country.

At this time the Swiss were trying to create a confederation. After many attempts, they were finally quite frustrated and discouraged at their lack of success. A long and bloody civil war seemed certain. The Swiss people were practically without hope.

Once Brother Klaus learned of this danger, he came to the conference in Zurich where the deliberations were being finalized. He found the conference room, sat in the back of the hall, and said nothing. Despite his quiet manner his presence was felt by all. The deliberations continued for many hours.

Finally, to the surprise of all, compromises were made on both sides. The modern Swiss federation was formed with all parties being satisfied. The presence of Brother Klaus made the difference. His presence permeated the hearts and minds of all present. Without uttering a word he changed the course of Swiss history. Deep holiness generates, in an almost silent way, betterment for all mankind.

Traversing the inner regions of the soul in a painfully truthful manner gradually causes one to discover profound interior healing and holiness. Michael, a young man in his late twenties, encountered God through a very powerful inner experience. After many months of therapy Michael finally came to a point of resolution regarding his relationship with his father.

During his formative years Michael's relationship with his father was null and void. They had no interchange and no communication. Michael knew his father only as another person who occupied a bedroom in the same house that he did. Complete estrangement and alienation characterized their relationship.

All of this left Michael in desperate straits as a male. Ideally, the father provides a sense of masculinity for the son. With this comes a feeling of confidence and mastery with regard to the world and its challenges. The father helps the son to deal with the challenges of life in a very straightforward manner. All of this Michael lacked.

After many months of sorting through feelings of rage and despair regarding his father Michael had a dream. In this dream he was swimming very deeply in the ocean. He noticed a very large white fish swimming next to him. This fish was practically the size of a whale. It was luminescent white. It glowed with life and warmth.

Michael's many months of trepidation regarding the inner journey finally ceased. He realized that he had paid the price and found healing. He was willing to undergo whatever pain was necessary in order to find the spirit of God within him. The fish symbolized Christ Jesus and his life-giving power. Never before had Michael encountered God in such a numinous manner. Wading through deep pain brought Michael into deep waters that transported him into the depths of the mystery of Christ in him and into the hope of glory.

I saw Michael about one year later. He was now progressing very well in school. He had a clear idea with regard to his vocational goals and his ability to attain them. In all ways, he genuinely felt confident and assured interiorly. He uncovered the mystery of the source of all life and healing—Christ Jesus, the Lord.

Deep movement into the presence of Jesus characterizes the mystery of Christianity. The spirit of God moves into the hearts of men and women during the depths of prayer and contemplation. In fact, monastic Christianity attempted always to devote a maximum amount of time to daily prayer.

The story is told of a Roman monk named Christopher of the monastery of St. Theodosius in Palestine. A young monk asked Christopher a question concerning the importance of deep prayer in spiritual formation. Christopher answered,

"My son, when I renounced the world, I was filled with a most intense ardor for the monastic life. By day I would busy myself as the rule prescribed and by night I would withdraw to the grotto which holds the tomb of St. Theodosius and the other fathers in order to pray there. As I descended to the grotto, I made a hundred genuflections to God on each of the eighteen steps. And when I had gone down all the steps, I stayed there until the bell rang; then I went up to attend the office. For ten years I lived like this, in fasting, in strict continence and in manual labor. Then one night I went down into the grotto as usual, making my genuflections on each step. When I reached the floor of the grotto, I was rapt into ecstasy and saw the whole floor of the grotto covered with candles. Some of these were burning, others were not. Then I saw two men clothed in white cloaks busying themselves with the candles. I asked them, 'Why are you arranging those candles? Why don't you go away and let me pray here?' They answered me, 'These are the candles of the fathers.' I asked again, 'Why are some burning and others not?' They replied again, 'Those who have wanted to do so have lit their candles.' Then I said to them, 'Tell me please, is my candle lit?' 'If you pray,' they said, 'we will light it.' I answered almost indignantly, 'Pray! What else have I been doing all this time?' Saying these words, I came to myself again and when I looked around, there was no one there."

Another example of this can be found in the life of St. Melanie the Younger:

With divine love . . . she would have liked to lock herself up in a cell away from everyone in order to give herself to uninterrupted prayer and fasting. This was impossible because of the many who found profit in her inspired teaching and constantly came asking for it. So she set aside certain hours, known to everyone, when she would make herself available for the benefit of the visitors, and the rest of the day she consecrated entirely to spiritual activities and dialogue with God in prayer.

The fruit of deep prayer is experiencing communion with God. Whether a soul is rapt in ecstasy or encounters the living God in and through a dream, God is in fact met in a personal manner. A genuine encounter with the risen Jesus produces changes deep inside the soul that are reflected in outer circumstances.

3

Holiness and Mental Health

Nothing Stands Between My Soul and My Savior

Genuine interior freedom and mental health result from a willingness to abandon one's ego totally and completely to God. In so doing, nothing interferes with personal, spiritual, and emotional well-being. In this state, God is totally in you and you are totally in God, a consummate immersion in deep prayer.

St. Paul, in his letter to the Philippians, states, "But whatever gain I had, I counted as loss for the sake of Christ" (3:7). Anything and everything, no matter how naturally appealing, must be considered loss for the sake of Christ. This allows nothing to stand in the way of one's relationship to the Divine. Such complete forsaking of all save Jesus cultivates true interior wholeness.

This is not to say that the things of this world and the goods of this world are to be despised and looked upon as evil. The danger with a black-and-white approach of this sort lies in developing an egocentric attitude that "It's me and Jesus, and the rest of the world is lost." Rather than seeing that this world was created by God and can indeed foster a relationship with Him, looking upon it as forsaken and devoid of His presence sets up a great deal of inner conflict. We would constantly feel ourselves to be at odds with our surroundings. Individuals in this sort of framework are prone to see a devil behind every rock. They are constantly on the lookout for sin, ungodliness, and evil. Since this a major preoccupation, they usually find what they are looking for, which only serves to confirm the whole vicious cycle.

Authentic mental health regards all that God has created as good and in some way purposeful. God is experienced as the source of all true well-being. Thus, the world, the thoughts and ideas that are

generated in this world, and even the material benefits of our
modern-day age are considered to be part of the synthetic whole of
God's work in creation. God is the source of all that is creative and
life-giving. All things work together in harmony to further the individual's communion with God.

The integration of one's interior being with the God of all the universe is at the heart of the Christian life. Nothing is permitted to
inhibit this natural flow. For this reason, St. Paul proclaimed, "Indeed I count everything as loss because of the surpassing worth of
knowing Christ Jesus my Lord . . . " (Phil. 3:8).

In a conversation with a Christian scholar, I was told, "The uni-
versal journey of the human soul toward God can be characterized by
one word—relinquishment. It requires the letting go of personal desires, ambitions, and possessions. Anything that would interfere with
the single-hearted devotion to Him, He gradually woos from us. The
surprising thing is that I find that I am most happy when I am preoccupied only by Him."

An anonymous fifteenth-century poet beautifully wrote:

> Thou shalt know Him when He comes
> Not by any din of drums—
> Nor the vantage of His airs—
> Nor by anything He wears—
> Neither by His crown—
> nor His gown,
> For His presence known shall be
> by the Holy Harmony
> That His coming makes in thee.

Thus, forsaking all for the sake of Christ creates new life in the
soul. A holy harmony heals the conflict-ridden personality. Releasing
yourself wholly to God readies your soul for holy harmony. The indescribable contentment of deep prayer embraces those who can genuinely proclaim, "Nothing stands between my soul and my savior."

Break the Misery Mood

"Finally, my brother, rejoice in the Lord" (Phil. 3:1). St. Paul's ex-
hortation was designed as a potent preventative for the early Chris-

tians' tendency to become entangled in false teaching. A separate group within the church wanted to impose stiff requirements on all Gentiles before allowing them to become Christians. This conflict generated enormous internal dissension in the church.

The great apostle to the Gentiles, St. Paul, had already experienced plenty of misery inflicted by others. The first chapter of Philippians records that he encountered individuals who preached the gospel out of envy, rivalry, and selfish ambition. In so doing, they hoped to increase Paul's persecution and personal misery. St. Paul, however, refused to buckle under the situation.

Human nature seems to have a predisposition toward misery. Quite often bickering, gossiping, and moodiness seem to be much easier to fall into than more positive and life-giving emotions are to cultivate. The misery habit plagues humankind. One misery after another seems to afflict a great many souls.

I remember a young woman talking with me one evening after a conference about the misery of her life. She said, "I notice that I am particularly miserable on two days, Tuesdays and Thursdays. When I looked into the matter, I realized that on Tuesdays and Thursdays I play tennis with seven other women. Once we are on the tennis court all of the horrible and chronic pains, problems and difficulties of everybody's life are brought up. One woman complains about her son who isn't making the grades that he could be making. The other woman complains about her husband who works too much. Another woman incessantly gripes about her in-laws. This goes on and on, week after week. They don't want to get out of their problems. They only want to commiserate with someone who will let them continue to feed off of their misery. They love to speak about how miserable and awful things are for them.

"What happens for me is that I end up miserable. I always feel horrible after our tennis games. I finally had to ask myself why I continue playing with these women. A funny thing came to mind.

"Somewhere deep down on the inside of me, I felt that the more miserable I was, the closer I was to God. Every Tuesday and Thursday after tennis, I felt so horrible that I would just take a hot bath and talk to God. I felt so close to Him during those times. I associated being miserable with being close to God. All that misery was the only thing that would drive me to my knees, so to speak.

"Once this dawned on me, the absurdity of it all became very apparent. I can turn to God at any time and feel close to Him. I don't need to wait until I feel miserable. The long and the short of it is that I lost seven tennis partners and I gained my mental health."

Breaking the misery habit demands that we can call into question those relationships and activities that might be perpetuating this negative cycle. People cause people to feel healthy or sick. People can cause you to feel happy or miserable. When you change your relationships and develop friendships with those who are trustworthy and positive, you take the first step toward breaking the misery habit. You will feel better about yourself, your friendships, and your personal relationship with God.

It has frequently been the case that in Christian circles suffering is viewed as quite holy. In relation to mental health, the holiness or pathology of suffering depends on the context. Suffering may or may not be redemptive.

The weight of depressive moodiness usually does not promote mental and spiritual health. Depressive symptoms that contort the psyche result from a giving in to the troublesome moods surrounding difficult outer circumstances. In other cases, the individual may be prone toward reacting with chronic states of moodiness and melancholia to a great many situations.

Meaningless depression results from falling under the weight of self-pity, emotional suppression, and a general reluctance to face truth. Unpleasant feelings are always the bearers of a potential for increased self-understanding. If the light and pain of this self-understanding is avoided, moodiness and depression ensue.

The daily occurrences of rejection, hurt feelings, resentments, frustrations, and guilt may all be used to further the growth of the soul. They act as the training ground for spiritual and psychological development. To embrace these sorts of sufferings and learn from them means to die to egocentric and selfish behaviors and attitudes. The cure, then, for poor mental health lies in the acceptance of real suffering.

Many contemporary views propose that the only way out of neurotic misery is to puff oneself up with happy feelings and thoughts. In reality this serves only to mask the need for real suffering. Colluding with the philosophy of eternal optimism stunts growth. When pain is not permitted, growth is not forthcoming.

The longing for freedom and growth can be satisfied only by paying the price of suffering and death to egocentric concerns and demands. You are not the center of the universe. All things do not occur in a manner pleasing to you all the time. God and His ways are at the heart of the universe. As we die to ourselves and live to Him, we break the misery habit.

As previously noted, death to egocentricities requires relinquishing attachments to miserable people and miserable moods. This is not to say that we stop extending ourselves to others in need. Rather, it is of utmost importance to discern those who are genuinely in need of our understanding and those who want another log added to the blazing furnace of their self-pity and bitterness. Such a differentiation aids us in the process of becoming healthier mentally and spiritually.

In a recent seminar, my wife provided a very excellent example regarding the importance of abandoning prolonged contact with chronically miserable people. She told the story of the feeding habits of the bears in Yellowstone Park. Evidently the bears dine freely and uninterruptedly before any of the other animals in the park. They have the choicest of sites at the best point of the local watering hole. No one disturbs the bears. Their ferocity commands that they be left utterly and serenely alone.

Only the skunk dares to partake side by side with the bears. Such unabashed courage on the part of the skunk has its reasons. The bears dare not tangle with the skunk, lest a foul odor be sprayed all over them. For days on end, a putrid stench would cover the bear and make him unacceptable to other bears. The bears know better than to mess with such an odor-ridden creature as the skunk.

My wife commented, "Miserable people are somewhat like skunks. Offering them a shoulder to cry on seems fine for the moment. Soon you will discover that no amount of understanding consoles them. They are intent on misery. And, sooner or later, you will do something to offend them, just as everyone else in their life has. You will then be sprayed with the odor of misery that will linger for days. A vague unhappiness will settle into your soul and a black cloud will seem to follow you wherever you go. Distress will be your lot for these days. It is best to love such people from a distance until they decide to allow our understanding to console them and help them release their misery."

The affliction of misery consumes the soul and darkens one's relationship to God. Unhappiness and dread seem to infect every square inch of one's inner being. The sweet presence of God drifts and drifts, farther and farther away. Misery can stand between your soul and your Savior.

Breaking the misery habit by foregoing miserable relationships and refusing to be swept away by the tide of negative moods accentuates spiritual vitality. Without misery, the soul is unencumbered in soaring onward toward God. The end of the misery habit signals the beginning of a new life. With misery left behind personal creative energies are freed to enter into the depths of prayer. Encountering God in deep prayer forever woos the soul away from the misery addiction and toward holiness, happiness, and health.

Cultivate the Happiness Habit

Happiness is, perhaps, the underlying motivator behind all of our activities and aspirations. Without happiness, life trudges on. Futility and emptiness plague unhappy souls. The yearning for fulfillment and happiness in work, relationships, and spirituality primes the pump for continued personal growth.

Happiness is not a frivolous and superficial emotion. One person told me, "I never talk about being happy. I consider happiness a flighty and vaporous sort of feeling. There's really not much to happiness. I've never really felt happy and I don't believe anyone else ever has." Unfortunately, his glib reply exposed a personal vacuum of terrifying immensity.

Bona fide emotional and spiritual happiness can pour forth continually from your soul as water from a deeply dug well. True happiness flows without contrivance or strain. Even in the midst of pain and turmoil, it runs ever steadily. It knows no highs or lows. Happiness flows from the innermost core of your being, despite outer circumstances.

When the times are good and you feel elated, and the times are bad and you feel depressed, being tossed to and fro with every gust of mood, you are far from happy. Situations in the outer world will always take a downturn at some point or another. At other times, everything will seem to go your way. Your happiness need not depend on the ups and downs of life.

The cultivation of a happiness that moves ahead despite daily plights challenges the believer. Great courage and steadfastness must come forth from within in order to engage in such an endeavor. Interior work, such as prayer and self-reflection, prepare the ground of

your heart for the harvest of happiness. With much personal diligence and the reign of God's blessing, happiness springs forth ready to
provide spiritual and emotional nourishment.

I am struck by St. Paul's implicit message regarding the emergence
of personal happiness. Before sharing his joy with the Philippians in
chapter three of his letter, he wrote about Timothy and Epaphroditus.
Paul's deep love for both of these men nurtured his joy in the Lord.

As St. Paul recorded,

> I hope in the Lord Jesus to send Timothy to you soon, that I may be
> cheered by news of you. I have no one like him, who will be genuinely
> anxious for your welfare. They all look after their own interests, not
> those of Jesus Christ. But Timothy's worth you know, how as a son with
> a father, he has served with me in the gospel. I hope therefore to send
> him just as soon as I see how it will go with me; and I trust in the Lord
> that shortly I myself shall come also. (2:19–24)

Paul knew Timothy so intimately that he could assuredly refer to
him as one who takes genuine interest in the welfare of other people.
Paul and Timothy shared a genuine relationship of deep concern for
each other. Timothy had proven himself to Paul. Paul had proven
himself to Timothy. They trusted each other. Paul cultivated his relationship with Timothy as a father with a son.

St. Paul then writes about Epaphroditus:

> I have thought it necessary to send to you Epaphroditus my brother and
> fellow worker and fellow soldier, and your messenger and minister to my
> need, for he has been longing for you all, and has been distressed be-
> cause you heard he was ill. Indeed he was ill, near to death. But God
> had mercy on him, and not only on him but on me also, lest I should
> have sorrow upon sorrow. I am the more eager to send him, therefore,
> that you may rejoice at seeing him again, and that I may be less anxious.
> So receive him in the Lord with all joy; and honor such men, for he
> nearly died for the work of Christ, risking his life to complete your ser-
> vice to me. (Phil. 2:25–30)

Once again Paul speaks from his heart about the importance of
personal relationships. Epaphroditus risked his life to take care of
Paul. Paul remarks that great sorrow would have engulfed him had
Epaphroditus died. A deep kinship of soul existed between Paul and
Epaphroditus.

The great apostle to the Gentiles had earlier remarked to the Philippians that he felt intimate communion with them as well:

> I thank my God in all my remembrance of you, always in every prayer of mine for you all making my prayer with joy, thankful for your partnership in the gospel from the first day until now. And I am sure that he who began a good work in you will bring it to completion at the day of Jesus Christ. It is right for me to feel thus about you all, because I hold you in my heart. (Phil. 1:3–7)

The great joy of Paul the apostle reflects his intimacy of relationship with Jesus and fellow believers. Spiritual relationships with friends who live deep in God create contentment and happiness of soul. Quality relationships, such as Paul knew with both Timothy and Epaphroditus, exemplify the fact that a kindred spirit lives in all those seeking to live deeply in God. A shared richness of spirituality encourages trust and caring to flourish. Happiness follows as a matter of course.

Attunement to cultivating positive personal relationships with others and with God promotes health of body, mind, and soul. The soul that can confidently affirm in the words of Jesus, "I and the Father are one," has found the interior spring of healing. Oneness with the Father can only be attained in and through the gradual working out of healthy relationships on this earth. True union with God is manifested concretely in union with others.

The foundation for wholeness, psychologically and spiritually, is laid in relationships, both human and divine. Diseases of the mind are rendered impotent once this bedrock is established. No matter the momentary turmoil of pain, the influx of the divine breath into the human soul and the loving concern from another person plant one's feet on the solid ground of love.

One of my analytic supervisors guided me in this matter, "As you remain close to God and close to those that care most about you, you will be able to carry on with your profession and ministry of healing without weariness and fatigue. During my early years I was frequently at odds with everyone around me. I ended up feeling sickly a great deal of the time. At one point, I even considered giving up my healing profession altogether. Once I discontinued living so separately from God and all my loved ones, a divine energy began to accompany me daily. It has been fifteen years since that moment of conversion.

"During those fifteen years, I have worked steadily as a psychotherapist without any extended vacation. I can truthfully say that never have I been afflicted by even a moment of debilitating pain or fatigue. I was so prone to this before. Even though I am constantly encountering extreme weakness, conflict, and illness in my patients, I am not infected. This makes sense to me. How could I be sick? How could a part of God be sick? Truly, greater is He that is in me than he that is in the world. I am happy, indeed, very happy."

God Is Here for You Now

The development of happiness and of peace of soul encourages the moment-to-moment experience of God's presence in the now. Rather than anticipating some future encounter with God, the believer maintains a constant awareness of His abiding embrace. Each moment of the day provides a unique opportunity to settle into God. As this occurs, the mind becomes freer and healthier.

St. Paul inspired the early church to cultivate mental freedom as he wrote: "Finally, brethren, whatever is true, whatever is honorable, whatever is just, whatever is pure, whatever is lovely, whatever is gracious, if there is any excellence, if there is anything worthy of praise, think about these things. What you have learned and received and heard and seen in me, do; and the God of peace will be with you" (Phil. 4:8–9).

That which preoccupies the mind shapes the person. Negative thoughts, dwelt upon over and over, create ungodliness and disease. Mental health sinks as destructive and negative ideas capture the imagination. God's presence and debilitating attitudes never mix. The more noncreative and demanding the thoughts, the more distance is created between the soul and God.

Fundamentally, God's presence always creates and makes all things new. He is the one who heals and restores the human heart. Even though His messages at times may be painful, the wound never results in spiritual death. God communicates love and life. Constructive, convicting, and inspiring ideas and thoughts issue forth from His mind to yours.

In the words of St. John Vianney, "Those who are led by the Holy Spirit have true ideas; that is why so many ignorant people are wiser than the learned. The Holy Spirit is light and strength."

Blessed Angela of Foligno further clarifies this matter:

> When the soul is illumined by the presence of God and doth repose in
> God's bosom and God in it, then is it exulted above itself and heareth
> and rejoiceth and doth rest in that divine goodness, concerning which
> none can report because it is above all intelligence and all manner of
> speech and above all words. But herein doth the soul swim in joyfulness
> and in knowledge, and thus enlightened, it comprehendeth the meaning
> of all the difficult and obscure sayings of Christ.

The mind functions using thoughts and images. Thoughts flow
through the mind in the form of statements about self, others, or the
world. Concurrently with this, images in the form of interior visual
representations play a major role in mental activity.

Purposely dwelling on positive thoughts, as encouraged by St. Paul,
assists the individual in spiritual growth, provided that such thoughts
come from God's inspiration as opposed to egocentered aspirations.
An egocentered approach to dwelling on positive thoughts, even
though the thoughts themselves may be very biblical, poses great
danger to the life of the soul. Satan himself quoted scripture to Jesus
in an attempt to sway Jesus away from God's plan. Scriptures and
positive thinking can be used for selfish ends. When this happens,
magic rather than the power of God moves the soul.

Timothy, a family man, well respected and loved in his community,
fell into the trap of using what we will call magic rather than the
power of God. He had been threatened with being laid off from work
for at least eighteen months. Throughout this time, he impulsively
decided that God surely did not will this layoff. He therefore stormed
the heavens through prayer and Bible-reading in order to ensure his
employment. Every morning, noon, and night he recited the verse,
"Now faith is the assurance of things hoped for, the conviction of
things not seen" (Heb. 11:1).

Dwelling on this verse fortified him mentally, but in a very egocentered fashion. The subconscious mind always responds to positive
or negative declarations, especially through constant repetition. As
he repeated this verse over and over and over, his ego became stronger and stronger. In subtle ways, this empowered him to manipulate
the external circumstances to such an extent that he never suffered
the loss of employment. He maintained his job. He also developed

chronic ulcers and feelings of intermittent anxiety. Using positive thoughts or scriptural verses for egocentric reasons always bears bad fruit.

Throughout all of this time, oddly enough, he had never directly sought God with regard to whether or not he should maintain his employment. He took for granted God's will for his life. Without ever praying about the matter and humbling himself to seek God, he fell prey to egocentricity. This left him a mess emotionally, spiritually, and physically.

Finally, some months later, he asked others to pray with him. A number of his friends confirmed a mutual feeling that perhaps he needed to let go of this job. He felt relieved and willing to respond. Two weeks later, his supervisor informed him of the coming layoff. He willingly acquiesced. A few weeks after this, it suddenly dawned upon him that he would now be able to finish his college degree. For several years, he had postponed completing his bachelor's degree because of his heavy work schedule. He lacked only six hours of course work to complete the degree.

Within six months he had completed the degree and was hired for a government position. This afforded him a unique opportunity for upward advancement as well as an immediate 30 percent pay increase. Resisting the will of God for an entire year through seemingly positive means had battered him physically and mentally. He had learned a very painful lesson about the importance of humbly seeking God and never presuming to know His will.

As he described it to me, "After I prayed with my friends, they offered to me the scripture from Isaiah that states, 'I will never leave you or forsake you.' This served to inspire and strengthen me in God's way. In the past, I had been using positive affirmations and scriptures so that I could get my way. Once I discerned what God really wanted, I felt free. Everything came together."

Images also exert a powerful influence on mental life. Scenes of various sorts, much like a motion picture, frequently accompany thoughts. If I ask you to think of an orange, in all likelihood you will have a mental representation of an orange in your mind. In other words, you will "see" an orange.

Symbols and images that emerge from the unconscious most powerfully influence the soul. They convey truths with great richness and simplicity. Symbols such as the pearl of great price, the mustard seed, the cross, or the Son of Righteousness rising with healing in His wing all depict very powerful images used throughout the scriptures. Such images evoke God's presence.

During her afternoon prayer time my wife Kathy quite spontaneously experienced an image of a ringing bell. This bell reminded her of the presence of God, felt during prayer. As she prayed, she had a clear visual representation of a bell. Now, whenever she recalls that bell or the memory of it emerges spontaneously, she feels drawn toward prayer. This image inspires her life of seeking union with God.

In fact, throughout the day, no matter what she is doing, the image of the bell soothes and settles her. One afternoon at lunch she remarked, "No matter how hectic the day or how tired I feel, the remembrance of the bell inspires me. It draws me closer to Him. It calls me to Him."

Dwelling on God-given images, such as the image of the bell, nurtures healing of mind and spirit. It transmits God's presence. Once the soul knows the reality of God, healing ensues. Knowing that GOD IS HERE FOR YOU NOW secures your soul in the reality of His loving embrace.

One Friday afternoon after having taught a Bible study group, I suggested to the participants that all of them imagine a bright sun shining from their chest and abdominal area. Earlier that day in prayer, I saw the image of the sun shining brightly within me. From this image, I sensed great warmth and healing.

Frequently I sense different inspirations right before teaching. These interior urgings frequently are God's way of telling me what His people need to hear. On that day, as the image of the bright and shining sun came to me, I passed on what I felt to be the image or symbol that would convey God's healing presence for His people.

As the participants closed their eyes, imagining the sun shining brightly within them, we prayed together. We prayed that healing would be felt in their spirit, mind, and body. As we stood together in the presence of God, His grace reached into the depths of our being through this image. Minds were cleared, attitudes uplifted, and bodies soothed and relaxed.

The following week, a woman shared with me, "Every day after Friday I felt God's presence stronger than ever before. Whenever I thought of the sun shining brightly within me, a strength seemed to be unleashed on the inside of me. A new sense of confidence and well-being came out of me. Even now, when I close my eyes and think about the sun shining within me, I sense God's presence."

Would you take a moment with me right now to experience the reality that GOD IS HERE FOR YOU NOW? For just a few moments we will, together, allow the warmth of His healing touch to settle on us. Allow Jesus to be here for you now by focusing on the image of the sun shining brightly within you.

Sit down in an easy chair and follow along with me. Gently close your eyes. As your eyes are closed, be aware of all the sounds in the room. Be aware of the feeling of the air on your skin. Be aware of your body breathing very gently and naturally on its own.

Now imagine the sun shining brightly from within you. Its rays are warm and bright. The rays extend down to your feet and toes and up to your arms, your hands, and your face. The warmth of the sun fills you.

Now as you imagine the sun warming you from within, repeat with me, "And now the Son of Righteousness rises with healing in His wings. And now the Son of Righteousness rises with healing in His wings. And now the Son of Righteousness rises with healing in His wings."

Repeat this scripture from Malachi 4:2 at least four times very, very slowly and meditatively. This image of the sun, together with the positive affirmation of scripture, instills healing in your mind. The Son of God, Jesus, acts on His word by your very utterance. Healing flows through your being by the power of His word. Jesus, the Son of Righteousness, has risen for you with healing in His wings.

Many have described mental healing as a feeling of great clarity and tranquillity of mind. Oftentimes this mental settledness affects the body in a very healing manner. You may notice that not only does your mind feel clearer and rested, but that your body also feels restored and refreshed. God is here for you now. He is the Son of Righteousness with healing in His wings for you.

Sheer Grace

The deliberate evolution of a relationship of nurturance with God and others strips the soul of falsity and pretensions, readying it for sheer grace. St. John of the Cross's concept of sheer grace illuminates the unique and true aspects of God's creative love. His continual act of creation in the human soul ushers one speedily into the Divine Presence.

Those moments of darkness, despair, and desolation are moments of sheer grace. God works in the soul to expose darkness and to move one from a position of egocentricity to God-centeredness. As we live in the Father's truth, moments of sheer grace multiply and mental health consequently increases.

Spiritual and mental purgation often confront the individual with dark terrors lurking within. In depth psychology, especially that school that stresses the unconscious import of relationships, the deepest terror of all is that of feeling utterly and completely alone in a hostile universe. The finger of a vengeful God points and declares, "You are guilty." The core of the psyche reverberates with this fear. It gnaws away at mental and spiritual health. It necessitates that the soul enter purgation, the dark night, in which the Father circumcises and liberates. The sacred scriptures refer time and time again to the needfulness of spiritual circumcision:

> Circumcise therefore the foreskin of you heart, and be no longer stubborn. (Deut. 10:16)
> And the Lord your God will circumcise your heart and the heart of your offspring, so that you will love the Lord your God with all your heart and with all your soul, that you may live. (Deut. 30:6)
> Circumcise yourselves to the Lord, remove the foreskin of your hearts, O men of Judah and inhabitants of Jerusalem; lest your wrath go forth like fire, and burn with none to quench it, because of the evil of your doings. (Jer. 4:4)
> He is a Jew who is one inwardly, and real circumcision is a matter of the heart, spiritual and not literal. His praise is not from men but from God. (Rom. 2:29)
> In him you were also circumcised with a circumcision made without hands, by putting off the body of flesh in the circumcision of Christ; and you were buried with him in baptism, in which you were also raised with him through faith in the working of God, who raised him from the dead. (Col. 2:11–12)

Many believers tremble at the thought of confronting interior desolation. Positive thinking and affirmation may be used to suppress unwanted feelings. By so denying our own dark despairings, we collude with the forces of darkness. Untruth maintains the soul in a state of oppression and bondage.

Jesus proclaimed, "I am the way, the truth, and the life." God is a God of truth, not of denial and suppression. All manner of truth eventually carries us to Him. Such truth may indeed be painful and frightening, but this wounding circumcises the heart of unconscious, nefarious elements. All truth comes from God and leads to God.

Personal frailties need not be stored away in a dark closet. God desires that all elements of your life be vulnerably exposed in His healing light. He does not cast us away for weakness. Human ineptitudes, candidly admitted in His presence, release the healing force of integration within the soul. Thus, in our weakness we become strong.

In the evenings, my wife and I usually read bedtime stories to our children. One night, after settling the children into bed, my wife Kathy read the children's story entitled, "The Little Tree and His Wish." I was captivated by its simplicity and heartwarming insight into human nature.

As the story goes, a very sad little tree moaned to all the forest animals that he was scrawny, little, and unappealing. He cried, "Nobody wants me. I'm scrawny and little and my wood is not very good."

Even though all the trees of the forest assured the little tree of their love for him, he would not listen. He wanted to be a big tree that would be chopped down and made into a sturdy wall, or be used in a magnificent home, or perhaps made into a fine table or boat. He did not realize how important he was as a little tree. All the birds built nests in his branches. He provided shade for little children on hot afternoons. All the animals loved him.

One day, a little old man went into the forest to find just the right tree for what he needed to build. He spotted the little tree and said, "Yes, yes, this is the tree I want. This wood will be all right." The little tree could hardly believe his ears. He wondered if he would be a table, a chair, or perhaps even a treasure chest. Needless to say, he was extremely excited and happy.

Once the old man arrived at home with the little tree, he began to prepare it for what he was about to construct. "Yes, sir," the little old man said, "you were mighty scrawny, but your wood will be all right for a manger. We need a sturdy manger to hold the hay for the cows." The little tree sighed, "But how I dreamed of palaces and kings!"

For many years, the little tree held the moist hay for the cows. One night, in a most unassuming manner, a man and a woman came to the little old man and asked for lodging. The old man offered his stable. As the man and his young, pregnant wife entered the stable, they spotted the manger. They spread soft hay along the inside of the manger. In a few hours, a beautiful baby boy lay in the manger. The little tree exclaimed with joy, "I like being a bed for a baby. The child is so warm and soft lying in the hay."

As the story continued, the stable soon filled up with shepherds and three kings. Angels were heard singing praises to God. The little tree listened as the shepherd prayed, "Thank you, dear Lord, for sending us your Son!"

The little tree thought, "This baby is God's Son! This baby is a king!" The story ends with the little tree thanking God that he could be the throne for such a very great king: "Thank you, dear God, for making me a scrawny little tree. Why, had I been a big and beautiful tree, I would never be the manger now!"

This little story helped my children to realize God's unconditional loving care for them. The Father deeply understands human misgivings and frailties. With full awareness of our imperfections, He loves us. In fact, the weaknesses and inadequacies that so trouble us actually potentiate His magnificence within us. Darkness, brought to light, is as a star shining in the heavens, radiating His splendor.

The moment of complete simplicity in which everything has been abandoned to Him, all darkness and all light, all weakness and all strength, is a moment of deep prayer. Interior circumcision of heart has occurred. The soul looks completely into Him and He into the soul. No separation exists between God and man. Holiness flows from the heart of the Divine to the heart of the human. Human and Divine become one.

This movement into sheer grace and deep prayer generates holiness and mental health. Very simply, the soul embraces the darkness of the moment only to encounter the presence of the living God. In the words of T. S. Eliot,

> Holiness is a condition of complete simplicity costing not less than everything.

Be Happy in the Moment

Embracing God in the moment causes one to be happy in the moment. All too often we look for happiness down the road somewhere. If only situations would change, if only this person or that would leave, if only work would improve, then happiness would be assured.

Waiting for happiness to come at some point in the future promotes great internal distress. We will be faced with happiness never coming. Happiness lies within you in the NOW.

Expecting happiness to come from the outside is similar to what St. Paul describes as placing confidence in the flesh. He writes, "If any other man thinks he has reason for confidence in the flesh, I have more: circumcised on the eighth day, of the people of Israel, of the tribe of Benjamin, a Hebrew born of Hebrews; as to the law a Pharisee, as to zeal a persecutor of the church, as to righteousness under the law blameless" (Phil. 3:4–6).

During my course of studies, fellow students were often convinced that they would find happiness once they had completed their Ph.D. One in particular remarked, "Once I have that Ph.D., I'll have it made. I can teach, work in a hospital, or work in private practice. I can call my own shots. I think that will make me plenty happy."

A number of years later, this same colleague recounted, "How naive I was. We never really have it made in life. Life's challenges keep coming up. It's best that I learn to be happy with what I have and who I am right now."

In church communities we find similar attitudes. A twenty-year-old college student told me, "If I didn't have to put up with all of my professors, do all this studying, and could just work full-time for the church, I'd be fully happy. Working for God full-time would be great. That's the next best thing to heaven. When I can do that, then I'll be really happy."

Within just a few months, this young man's dream came true. He was offered and he accepted a position involving full-time church work. He coordinated the various youth groups for the parish, organized the music for Sunday liturgies, and took care of general administrative responsibilities delegated by the pastor. Now he was working in heaven . . . or so he thought.

Three months into his job, he pulled me aside and said, "Working for the church is no cup of tea. There's problems here just like everywhere else. No one can agree on meeting times. One group wants this, another group that. Some parishioners like the music during Sunday Mass, others complain about it. At times even Father and I have disagreements. Working for the church full-time sure isn't the answer to the question of how to find happiness."

In the months to come, this young man stabilized in his life of prayer and matured in his spiritual attitude. He did, in fact, become happy in his work within the church. This happened not because of any lessening of church-related problems, but because of his willingness to be happy and cultivate his happiness each moment no matter where he was, no matter what he was doing. Psychologically, his mental struggles and conflicts decreased as he accepted himself and his situation in the moment.

Accepting your humanity in the moment sensitizes you to the presence of happiness in the moment. Difficulties and dilemmas are a part of life. They cannot be avoided. They are a part of being human and living in a human world.

God's grace builds on the humanity of each moment. The more you accept yourself, where you are and who you are in each moment, the more contented you grow. He is with you now, at this very moment, no matter what you are going through. No matter how you feel about yourself. His grace of happiness in the moment is here for you now.

On another night, Kathy shared with our children the fairy tale of "The Fir Tree" by Hans Christian Anderson, a story that illustrates the importance of being happy in the moment. In the forest stood a very pretty and small little fir tree. Everyone would comment on how tiny and beautiful it was. The fir tree did not appreciate these comments, for it wanted to be a big and great tree. The sunbeams told the fir tree, "Rejoice in your youth. Rejoice in your fresh growth and young life!"

The little fir tree did not understand and complained that it wanted to be bigger and better. At Christmas time he would notice all the large trees being cut down to be used as Christmas trees. His greatest desire was to be a large and grand Christmas tree.

Finally, one Christmas, his wish came true. He fell to the ground with a great sigh. "I thought I would feel happy to leave, but it is sad to leave my friends and my home." He was taken to a large house, placed in a tub filled with sand, and decorated with golden apples, walnuts, ribbons, and colored candles. The children danced around the tree, rushing about so forcefully that some of the branches bent and cracked. Feeling confused and sad, the tree asked, "What next?"

In the evenings he heard an old man tell the young children marvelous stories, all with happy endings. He thought, "Surely I will live happily ever after too." With all of the candles and ribbons that adorned him, he just knew that surely the other trees in the forest would be jealous if they could see him. He thought that surely now he would live happily ever after.

Soon the day came for the servants to remove the Christmas tree. They dragged him into the upstairs attic. Thrown in a dark corner, he asked, "What will happen to me now?" He remembered the forest and the animals that would come to play under his branches. He remembered how he complained about everything then. As time went on, his branches became yellow and brittle.

He reflected that he had always been looking for happiness in becoming bigger and better. Happiness always seemed to elude him. As he remembered his youth in the forest and Christmas Eve with the children, he realized that he had been happy all the time and never knew it. The old tree exclaimed, "I was happy and I never knew it! I always wanted something else. Now it's all past—gone forever!"

At the end of the story, my daughter Katherine remarked, "What a sad story." Kathy told her, "It's always sad when we don't let ourselves be happy every day. Life seems then to pass us by. You can be happy every day, Katherine, if you just let yourself be."

To be happy in the moment is living deep prayer. A soul at peace and content in the now abides under the wing of the Almighty. The believer is shielded and protected in the constancy of God's experienced presence.

In the words of the psalmist, "Because he cleaves to me in love, I will deliver him; I will protect him, because he knows my name. When he calls to me, I will answer him; I will be with him in trouble, I will rescue him and honor him. With long life I will satisfy him, and show him my salvation" (91:14–16).

Health and Past Pain

Health and happiness emerge from dealing with the past, not running from the past. All too easily, individuals discount past sufferings as dead and gone. I often hear, "The past is over. Put it behind you. You can't do anything about it. Just forget about it."

Unfortunately, past pains do not magically disappear. Emotions, past or present, generate tremendous internal energy. This intense emotional force resides latently in the soul, if not uncovered and worked through. The suppression of emotions forces them into unconsciousness and destructive modes of inadvertent expression.

Tom, a forty-three-year-old man who suffered from intense shyness
and insecurity, related his predicament to me. As a young boy in the
Midwest, he grew up as an only child on an isolated farm. During
the days he attended school while his parents worked the farm. In the
evenings, after completing his homework, he felt the pains of loneliness and emptiness. Both of his parents distanced themselves from
emotional closeness and affection.

His father would spend the entire evening behind a newspaper.
From 7:00 P.M. to 10:00 P.M. he read every word in the newspaper.
He uttered nothing and merely rocked back and forth in his rickety
rocking chair, evening after evening.

His mother crocheted the evening away. She never asked about
Tom's day or about his feelings. He recalled her as being "cold, unfeeling, like she lived on another planet."

At age eighteen, Tom finally left the farm. He enrolled in a college located in a nearby metropolis. There he cultivated friendships
and learned the meaning of human intimacy and warmth. By the end
of college, he had no desire to return to the farm. He lived and
worked in the big city.

Soon after his marriage, a major problem erupted. He felt pressure
from his parents to visit them, especially now that he was married
and would be starting a family. In his words, "They wanted to see
me, not so much because they felt close to me, but because it was the
thing to do. The family should stick together. I detested the thought
of returning on a regular basis to that farmhouse."

Soon, the mere sight of the farmhouse caused Tom to break out
into hives with uncontrollable feelings of nausea. His state worsened
to such a degree that he actually vomited numerous times during the
short drive to his parents' home. His symptoms left him drained and
confused. For so long, he felt that the past was behind him, dead and
gone.

Much to his surprise, his past lived on heartily in the depths of his
soul. Each instance of disgust and vomiting recalled past feelings of
emotional neglect and deprivation. Over a period of many months
Tom confronted and released these feelings. His symptoms disappeared. Tom regained health and wholeness from dealing with his
past, not running from his past.

I periodically reflect on the spiritual and emotional ordeal St. Paul
must have experienced after his conversion. As a zealous Jew, he per-
secuted and murdered scores of innocent people. The groanings of the

dying must have echoed through the recesses of his memory. On a purely psychological level, he could have been overwhelmed with the remorse and trauma of haunting voices and screams from his past. St. Paul knew the pains of emotional scarring.

Out of his own healed agony he wrote, "But our commonwealth is in heaven, and from it we await a Savior, the Lord Jesus Christ, who will change our lowly body to be like his glorious body, by the power which enables him even to subject all things to himself" (Phil. 3:20, 21). All things, including painful memories, come under the control of Christ Jesus. He is the healer of our woundedness.

Inner transformation comes from God. A yielded life produces a holiness that heals past psychological injuries. Gradually but deliberately a desire for health ushers forth memories of the past, and resolution and healing can result. A soul centered on God need have no fear of the past, for Christ Jesus brings everything under His control. When we tremble with fright, His strength within us stands unshaken. In our weakness, we can rely on Him.

I have found that many individuals are opposed to the study of psychology out of a personal fear of having to confront their past. Superficially they slight and demean even a Christian-based psychology. The louder they protest, the more they have to hide. One who ardently boasts of having no painful memories and not being in need of interior healing frequently needs the most help. The louder the outward protestation, the deeper the inward pain.

To further illustrate the necessity of resolving past conflicts in order to enable present and future spiritual growth, the case of a young religious brother comes to mind. As a man in his late thirties, he felt very committed to deepening his relationship with God. In his mind, the world offered nothing of lasting value. He greatly yearned to live deeply in God.

For five years he battled incessantly with alcoholism. Unknown to his superiors, he hid bottles of whiskey between his mattresses. During the afternoon and evening, he sipped away his cares and concerns. As time went on, his conscience troubled him more and more. He longed for God, but the addiction to alcohol enslaved him.

Time after time, he attempted to quit to no avail. Alcoholism thwarted his spiritual growth. This problem ravaged his interior life until one day when the truth finally emerged. After dinner with the other religious, he quietly escaped to his bedroom, reached between the mattresses for the liquor bottle, but failed to close the bedroom door completely. His superior walked by and witnessed his drinking.

Without any loss of time his superior lovingly but firmly confronted him. The brother remarked to me, "Finally I was caught. I wanted help and I needed treatment. I let myself be caught. It felt so good to have someone know and be concerned."

After one year of intensive treatment involving both in-patient and out-patient care, freedom took hold. As he recalled, "I learned why I felt so compelled to drink. It traced back to my early childhood years. Without knowing this, I was walking around with a ball and chain on both feet trying to grow spiritually and psychologically. It was impossible.

"When I was three, four, or five, somewhere around there, I distinctly remember my father pushing me away from the dinner table, where he was seated drinking with many of his buddies. He told me that I was too young to drink and shouldn't be around there. I felt intense rejection and pain. I ran to the bathroom. I wept and wept alone.

"Finally, a friend of my father's entered the bathroom, closing the door behind him. He picked me up and said, 'Since you aren't good enough to drink, I'll show you what you are good for.' He then proceeded to abuse me sexually. With his hand cupped over my mouth, I couldn't yell or scream. After he was finished, he said, 'You're good for that and you're good for this.' He raised me up, almost rolled me in a ball, lifted the lid of the toilet seat, and sank me into the bowl full of water and urine. He looked at me and said, 'If you tell anyone, I'll kill you.'

"I learned through that trauma that not drinking meant I was less than a man and no better than a pot full of urine. So, as I grew older, I drank and drank and drank. In some twisted way, I associated drinking with being strong like a man. Once I understood this, I knew what possessed me to drink. Without dealing with these past feelings, brutal enslavement to alcohol captivated me. After almost two years now, I feel better than before. I had to deal with my past before I could grow closer to God."

Working through past suppressed pains frees the soul to embrace the living presence of Jesus. Such an encounter characterizes deep prayer. Without incessant struggling, the soul, unencumbered by the weightiness of past traumas, lives in Him experientially during both quiet prayer and daily routine. St. Symeon, the New Theologian, profoundly described the spiritual unshackling that occurs with inner healing:

> Likewise that soul about which I am speaking, when it sees how the light shines, and knows that itself is completely in most terrible darkness and in this completely enclosed prison and most profound ignorance, then it sees just where it is lying, where it is locked in and that this place is completely a mudhole, full of slimy, poisonous snakes; that it itself is chained, both hands and feet bound by shackles and that it is covered with dust and filth; that it is also wounded from the bites of the reptiles and that its own flesh is puffed up and also covered with numerous worms. Seeing this, how will the soul not shudder? How will it not cry out? And ardently be repentant and beg to be rescued from such terrible fetters? Yes, all who see such indeed will lament and groan and will want to follow after Christ Who makes the light so radiant!

Letting Go on the Inside

Deep prayer and holiness create inner growth without conscious planning and deliberation. Indeed, a step-by-step approach to holiness and mental health sabotages its very development. Sanctity flows from within, without conscious contrivance. In the end, holiness and health involve letting go on the inside to God.

A Russian pilgrim in the book *The Way of a Pilgrim* relates his experience of deep prayer taking a hold of him on the inside:

> I became so accustomed to praying that if I stopped, even for a moment, I experienced a sense of emptiness, as if I had lost something. But as soon as I started again I became lighthearted and happy once more. I wanted to remain there alone—I had no desire to see anyone, and I was completely happy.
>
> When I went back to the staretz I described this joy to him, and after he had listened to me he said: "Now that you have made a habit of prayer, try to maintain that habit, and strengthen it. Never waste time, love solitude, rise early, and resolve to remain united to God."
>
> One morning early, I was, as it were, woken up by prayer. I began to say my morning prayers, but it was as if my tongue was tied, and I was overcome with the desire to simply repeat the Jesus Prayer. I began to repeat it and was immediately happy. My lips moved effortlessly, of their own accord.

I passed the whole of that day in a state of joy. It was as though I was detached from everything, and I felt as if I was in another world. I went to see the staretz and gave him a detailed account of all this. When I had finished, he said: "God has given you the desire to pray, and the capacity to do so without effort."

What heights of perfection, what ecstatic joy man can experience, when the Lord wishes to reveal the secrets of prayer to him and purify his passions! It is an indescribable state, and the revelation of this mystery is like a foretaste of the delights of heaven. This is the gift which they receive who seek the Lord with love and with singleness of heart.

Attachment to Him alone transforms the weary soul into a vibrant spirit.

In his letter to the Philippians, St. Paul writes,

> But whatever gain I had, I counted as loss for the sake of Christ. Indeed I count everything as loss because of the surpassing worth of knowing Christ Jesus my Lord. For his sake I have suffered the loss of all things, and count them as refuse, in order that I may gain Christ and be found in him, not having a righteousness of my own, based on law, but that which is through faith in Christ, the righteousness from God that depends on faith; that I may know him and the power of his resurrection, and may share his sufferings, becoming like him in his death, that if possible I may attain the resurrection from the dead. (3:7–11)

Counting all as loss for the sake of Christ means far more than external relinquishments. Although the Christian life demands the forsaking of material attachments, interior detachment must also be forthcoming. A young seminarian remarked, "Facing the prospect of celibacy seems simple on the outside; but can I live like a celibate on the inside? Will I be obsessed with women in my thought life? Will such an obsession eventually result in an indirect and destructive expression of my sexuality through pornography or illicit sexual involvements? If celibacy is my gift, then God will provide the grace for both inner and outer detachment."

In the words of Charles de Foucauld,

> Perfect trust demands a most lively and literal sense of God's reality, of His power, and of His benevolence. Of course, it is obvious that Perfect Wisdom can do much better for us than our own common sense, but it is easy in practice to forget this principle and try to be clever.

The most practical aspect of trust in Providence, for the saints, is tied to their commitment to poverty. If one relinquishes all material prudence, yet still undertakes great works, then God must provide everything necessary, at just the right moment. The annals of sainthood, ancient and modern, are full of accounts of everyone sitting down to dinner around an empty pot offering thanks, then answering a knock at the door to find a donor with an extra goose, or the equivalent, in hand. On a larger scale, the great founders and builders habitually sign contracts for thousands or millions, with no cash and no credit, and no anxiety either.

The best natural model of this virtue is the trust of infancy, which we once blissfully knew, before the discovery that human adults are not omnipotent or necessarily benevolent. " . . . whoever does not receive the kingdom of God like a child shall not enter it" (Mark 10:15).

Father, I abandon myself into your hands; do with me what you will. Whatever you may do, I thank you; I am ready for all, I accept all. But only your will be done in me and in all your creatures—I wish no more than this, Lord."

Letting go on the inside creates equanimity and peace of mind. One who trusts perfectly in God's providential care walks in the way that is holy. In the words of the psalmist, "Great peace have those who love thy law; nothing can make them stumble" (119:165).

A middle-aged Roman Catholic sister conveyed to me her conflict regarding traditional spiritual formation and her current spiritual mentality. For so long she had clung to her prayer books, external religious exercises, and outward observances of various sorts. More and more, these religious activities left her desolate and dry. Only intense interiority settled and soothed her soul.

In her words, "The old way doesn't seem to make much sense to me anymore. Reading prayers from books no longer touches me deeply. I need more and more quiet time alone with Him in silence. I come to know Him better when I am still within."

For five years, she struggled with letting go of customary religious practices. Only the experience of contemplative prayer nurtured and filled her soul. In order to stand in the presence of the Holy, even the familiar modes of prayer had to be forsaken. Only complete aloneness with the Great Alone satisfied her longing.

She reported, "Terror such as this I have never known. No one seemed to understand me. I was alone with God. Once I let go of all external attachments, I truly discovered God. He wants me and me alone."

Inner quietude and letting go culminate in a moment of deep prayer. When everything, conscious and unconscious, disengages from the mind, God's spirit flows freely. Sensitization to His presence increases with internal relaxation.

A Canadian psychiatrist, Dr. R. M. Buche, characterized his own experience of transcendent awareness by detailing the following account:

I had spent the evening in a great city with two friends, reading and discussing poetry and philosophy. We parted at midnight. I had a long drive in a hansom to my lodging. My mind, deeply under the influence of the ideas, images, and emotions called up by the reading and talk, was calm and peaceful. I was in a state of quiet, almost passive enjoyment, not actually thinking, but letting ideas, images, and emotions flow of themselves, as it were, through my mind. All at once, without warning of any kind, I found myself wrapped in a flame-colored cloud. For an instant I thought of fire, an immense conflagration somewhere close by in that great city; the next, I knew that the fire was within myself. Directly afterward, there came upon me a sense of exultation, of immense joyousness accompanied or immediately followed by an intellectual illumination impossible to describe. Among other things, I did not merely come to believe, but I saw that the universe is not composed of dead matter, but is, on the contrary, a living presence; I became conscious in my self of eternal life. It was not a conviction that I would have eternal life, but a consciousness that I possessed eternal life then; I saw that all men are immortal; that the cosmic order is such that without any peradventure all things work together for the good of each and all; that the foundation principle of the world, of all the worlds, is what we call love, and that the happiness of each and all is in the long run absolutely certain. The vision lasted a few seconds and was gone; but the memory of it and the sense of the reality of what it taught has remained during the quarter of the century which has since elapsed. I knew what the vision showed was true. I had attained a point of view from which I saw that it must be true. That view, that conviction, I may say that consciousness, has never, even during periods of the deepest depression, been lost.

Let Peace Stand Guard Over Your Heart

As past crises surface and heal, peace establishes itself in the heart. You do not manufacture peace. God freely bestows peace to those who love Him and follow His ways. You merely permit the unfolding development of peace to occur interiorly in an unobstructed manner. St. Paul, in his letter to the Philippians, sensitizes the Christian community as to the availability of peace:

> Rejoice in the Lord always; again I will say, Rejoice. Let all men know your forbearance. The Lord is at hand. Have no anxiety about anything, but in everything by prayer and supplication with thanksgiving let your requests by made known to God. And the peace of God, which passes all understanding, will keep your hearts and your minds in Christ Jesus. (4:4–7)

Peace stands guard like a sentry over the mind and the heart of the believer. Once again, God graciously gives peace to all those yielded to Him. This peace guards the mind and heart from anxiety and destructive emotions. It guards the soul from negativism and distress.

Peace watches over the mind by dispelling unwanted thoughts. The mind generates thoughts and ideas. Creative and positive ideas contribute to health and wholeness. Mentally yielding to negative thoughts cripples the soul. Attitudes such as, "I can't do it," "it will never get better," or "nothing ever goes my way" run rampant in the oppressed mind.

The heart, as the feeling function of the soul, understands and learns from dark emotions when peace stands guard. Negative feelings pass away once the individual integrates the lessons they bring. Without peace, an inundation of negative feelings overcomes the heart. Dwelling on the negative rather than feeling it and learning from it characterizes an anxiety-ridden personality. Only by allowing peace to maintain a watchfulness over the heart will emotional and spiritual health ensue.

St. Paul writes about both joy and gentleness in the context of his message on peace. Joy and gentleness branch out from the trunk of peace. When peace stands guard over the mind and heart, joy and gentleness accompany it.

John, a young banker, related to me how mightily he struggled with joy: "I always thought that I wanted to be happy. As I sorted through deep feelings of despair and loneliness from my past, I discovered more peace and also more joy. The joy frightened me.

"I had become used to black moods. In fact, they offered me comfort and solace. If I didn't feel like doing something, I had an excuse. I was feeling low and down. Who could blame me? I actually looked forward to these heavy feelings.

"Joy energized me and made me ready to approach life and my work wholeheartedly. This scared me to death. I no longer had an excuse to cop out. I was feeling good, in fact, joyful. I could hardly stand it.

"I remember for about three months actually trying to make myself feel depressed. If I felt good, then I had to apply myself all the way, to my work and to my relationships. I never had to give all of myself before. Somehow, no matter how hard I tried, I could no longer get the depression to stick with me. Having dealt with my past, the depression no longer could gain a foothold in my mind and heart. For a moment, I even considered it tragic that I now knew joy.

"Fortunately for me, this condition lasted for only two or three months. The rewards of living fully with joy surpassed any negative reasons I had for remaining depressed. Now I give myself wholeheartedly to everyone and everything that I am doing. I feel much better. Joy energized me to do this."

In this case, John purposefully attempted to dwell on negative thoughts and succumb to dark feelings. Peace guarded his heart so definitely that even his conscious negative contrivings could not break through. Real peace, like this, will stand guard over your mind and heart as you grow emotionally and spiritually. Joy will exude from within you and invigorate your work and relationships.

Along with joy, gentleness or littleness of heart arises out of bona fide inner tranquillity. The deep calm found in God's holy presence imbues the soul with humility. Such littleness of heart dissipates all anxious striving. Egocentric graspings no longer dominate the God-centered individual. He or she rests in an interior awareness of God's ever-present power.

Men, in particular, may find this virtue quite perplexing. Forcefulness and aggressivity plague modern men. The more neurotic the man, the more insensitivity and blatant aggression abound in him. The more he battles onward, attempting to conquer and gain that which he lusts after, the more interior disease infects him. The ego's unbridled forcefulness destroys relationships and corrupts the soul. It is no wonder that such men eventually feel that all of life is senseless, worthless, and for naught. They have invested themselves in mean-

ingless and selfish endeavors in order to fill up the canyon of emptiness within them. None of this satisfies. Hollowness and sterility
criple such souls.

The gentle way arises out of deep peacefulness. God, not man,
controls the forces of life. Such an awareness soothes the human
heart. Gentleness is the surest evidence of His power.

Spiritual and emotional health hinge on the formation of littleness
of heart. Herein the believer rests in the surety of God's everlasting
providence. A peaceful knowing courses through the mind and heart.
In this state of unity between the soul and God, the human heart
feels more and more saturated with God's own health and well-being.

God impressed upon me a new grace of littleness one afternoon
during my time of prayer. While in a state of settled contemplation,
an image arose from within me. This scene communicated, in a most
dramatic way, the importance of littleness and gentleness in facing
life's quandaries.

In this colorful scene, I stood on a sidewalk in the middle of a
residential neighborhood. Houses and trees lined the street. The sun
shone brightly in the blue sky. The air felt cool and fresh.

All of a sudden, I noticed a huge semitruck barreling down the
street. As I turned to my left, I noticed my little daughter at the
other end of the block right in the middle of the street sitting on a
skateboard. She just sat contentedly on this board while the truck
traveled at a high speed toward her. Paralysis gripped me. I could not
move.

Horror-stricken, I watched as the huge truck sped toward my
daughter. With the truck ten or fifteen feet away from her, my daughter gently lay back on the skateboard. When the truck came upon
her, she lay completely prostrate on the board. The truck swept over
her.

She emerged from under the truck. Completely unscathed, she
smiled at me. Owing to her lying completely flat on the skateboard,
she slid without harm under the chassis of the truck. Her littleness
protected her.

His voiceless voice spoke the words, "With great littleness you
avoid great disaster." He infused new grace into my being. In the days
and months to come, this grace activated gentleness and littleness
within me whenever disaster threatened. A newfound ease in coping
with life's constant predicaments dawned upon me. Littleness of heart
contributed to a greater constancy of interior peace.

Joy and littleness work hand in hand with peace. They promote the interior development of tranquillity and restfulness. In the midst of life's activities, peace stands guard over the mind and heart with the constant support of joy and littleness.

Everything Is as It Should Be

For the believer, all things work together for the good. The circumstances and people in your life at this present moment are purposely meant, in some way, to deepen your relationship with God. Each present moment calls you to live life more deeply. Feeling the full impact of each moment nourishes the believer with an awareness of God's presence.

This very moment is sacramental. It communicates God's essence in a singular manner. No other moment will be like this very moment. God orders each and every moment to heal and deepen you spiritually.

Thus, we as believers have the opportunity to rest content in the moment, trusting in God's deliberate caring. "I have learned the secret of facing plenty and hunger . . . " (Phil. 4:12). Contentment in the moment eventually dawns on one who seeks God. Throughout life, an individual can strive to attain some perfect time far off in the future. No such time exists. This is the perfect moment. Resting contentedly in this assurance fortifies spiritual and emotional health.

My son Paul convincingly demonstrated the importance of living fully in the present moment. Late one afternoon he asked Kathy if he might have a friend over to play. Our agreement with regard to having friends over is that schoolwork must first be completed before any entertaining can be done. He assured Kathy that he had completed his school assignments.

From four-thirty to six o'clock he and a friend played in our backyard. Shortly after supper, we all gathered together to work on a puzzle. I noticed that Paul had slipped off to the study by himself, very quietly. I followed him into the study and asked why he needed to do more work. He told me quite plainly that he still needed to complete his homework. He somehow had managed to forget to finish a few odds and ends. For the next hour and a half, he remained in the study, completing his homework.

Kathy finally checked on him. His eyes were red, his hair messed up, as he slumped into his chair. She looked over his homework and found six wrong answers. She pointed these out and offered to help him correct them. He looked at the wrong answers in disbelief and said, "I don't know what happened. When I wrote the answers down, they were right. I don't know how they got wrong." They finally corrected the answers and Paul ran off to bed.

Early the next morning he came into our bedroom and insightfully declared, "I guess it's best to do my homework when I have to do it. If I put it off, I can't think straight. Then I start complaining and getting grouchy. Right looks wrong and wrong looks right. From now on, I'm going to do things when I have to do them and not put them off."

Struggling against the requirements of the present moment creates unnecessary frustration and interior distress. God provides the necessary grace each moment to fulfill the task at hand. Putting off life's demands wastes the grace of the present moment. Wasted grace propagates psychological malaise. Responding to God's call in the moment, as manifested in practical daily situations, consumes the grace of the moment and readies the soul for a greater portion of new grace.

St. John of the Cross describes this perfect reliance upon God in the following manner:

> If you would come to taste all things;
>   then do not seek anything.
> If you would come to possess all things;
>   then do not seek to possess anything.
> If you would come to be everything;
>   then do not seek to be anything.
> If you would know everything;
>   then do not seek to know anything.
> To reach that for which you have no taste,
>   you have to go where you have no taste to go.
> To reach what you do not know,
>   you have to go where you do not know.
> To come to possess what you do not possess,
>   you have to go where you have no possessions.
> To reach what you are not,
>   you have to go where you are nothing.
> When you dwell on any one thing,
>   you cease to cast yourself upon the All.

> To pass from all things to the All,
>   you have to deny yourself wholly in all things.
> And when you come to have the All,
>   you must have it without asking for anything.
> For if you wish to have anything at all,
>   then you do not have your treasure surely in God.

Resting contentedly in God alone summarizes the purity of the Christian way. One lives deep prayer in this manner. Whether walking, sitting, talking, or reading, deep prayer fills the soul as God alone is the object of desire. At this moment, you have all that you need. You have God. Rest contentedly in the moment knowing that He is here for you.

Every present moment, for one surrendered to the Divine, is a moment with Him. St. Alonso told his confessor: "It has sometimes happened that, before going to bed, I have begun praying and continued to do so while at the same time I was fast asleep. And when I fall asleep I pray as I do when I am awake. I sleep, but my heart keeps watch."

With such a realization, mental health develops more consistently. Rather than anxiously striving for spiritual and psychological growth, one can more naturally abide in God's ever-present reality. He abides in all that you do. In wakefulness and in sleep, you are with Him and He is with you. Whether in formal prayer or in the routine of daily work, His presence guides you. He is always with you. Be at peace.

In accepting the present moment, we must surely realize that God loves us just the way we are but loves us too much to let us stay that way. That is to say, each circumstance in your present life potentially pulls you into greater personal development. It does not leave you stagnant. You, in the circumstances you are presently in, are not meant to remain the way you are now forever.

God's wholehearted acceptance of you right now, just the way you are, empowers you to yield yourself in a more trusting manner to Him. His creative power then works gradually and surely in the deepest recesses of your soul, promoting long-term and satisfying change. " . . . for God is at work in you, both to will and to work for his good pleasure" (Phil. 2:13).

God in you sees you through each moment in order that you may fulfill His divine purpose. From the moment of your conception, His blueprint for your life resided in your innermost being. Living fully each moment in His presence places you in harmony with His plan. A deep harmony with Him creates good spiritual fruit. Health of mind saturates the one who lives deeply in Him. It is Christ in you, the hope of glory, that emerges as the wellspring of all mental and spiritual well-being.

As Christ Jesus copenetrates the soul, a deep impression of His presence delicately embraces one in such a way that, in the words of St. John of the Cross, the soul

> . . . finds no terms, no means, no comparison whereby to render the sublimity of the wisdom and the delicacy of the spiritual feeling with which she is filled . . . we receive this mystical knowledge of God clothed in none of the kinds of images, and none of the sensible representations, which our mind makes use of in other circumstances. Accordingly, in this knowledge, since the senses and the imagination are not employed, we get neither form nor impression, nor can we give any account or furnish any likeness, although the mysterious and sweet-tasting wisdom comes home so clearly to the inmost parts of our soul.

Deep union with God through deep prayer heals the psyche, in that all discordant elements are unified. Every man and woman needs to feel whole and a sense of oneness within. A deeply felt encounter with God meets this need.

The door into the region of inner harmony lies wide open for those yielded to the spirit of God. In a moment of great revelation, Mary encountered the presence of the living God through the angel Gabriel. In this special moment she decided to relinquish her way of thinking about things and give herself over to God. " . . . Behold, I am the handmaid of the Lord; let it be to me according to your word" (Luke 1:38).

After this complete abandonment of herself to God, Mary proclaimed, "My soul magnifies the Lord, and my spirit rejoices in God my Savior, for he has regarded the low estate of his handmaiden." (Luke 1:46–48). Her entire being praised God. No discordant elements existed within her at that moment. Wholeness and holiness consumed her.

Mary then acknowledged her own experience of vulnerability and infilling: "He has filled the hungry with good things" (Luke 1:53). Mary's interior hunger to know God had been filled. The Word abided within her.

From Mary we learn of the potentiality that all of us can feel the Word alive within us. Jesus can heal your fractured soul. When you feel that you are coming apart at the seams, have nowhere to turn, and are ready to lose hold of your grip on life, know that He is with you. Surrender yourself totally, without reservation, to Him. Only in this manner can He heal your mind. Your anxious and divided mind can be brought together again. Your deepest need is to feel the whole of God in the whole of your soul. God will meet this need for you as you give yourself over to Him . . . in the now.

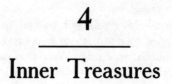

4

Inner Treasures

A Humble Heart Is a Holy Heart

The following story is told of the holy one who lived in the desert and prayed night and day:

> A girl in the fishing village became an unwed mother. After several beatings she finally revealed who the father of the child was: a holy man living far off in the desert.
>
> This holy man was known far and wide. All in the village revered him. They considered him to be a living saint.
>
> All of the villagers marched up to the holy man's house. They intruded upon him during his prayer, cursed him for being a hypocrite, and told him to now care for the baby. All the holy one said was, "I see. I see."
>
> He quickly made arrangements for the baby. He saw to it that a woman in the village, a woman that he trusted, cared for the little child. The woman then fed, clothed and loved the little baby, all at the expense of the holy one.
>
> The holy one was no longer considered a living saint. His reputation had been sullied. All of his followers left him.
>
> Finally, after a year, the mother of the child could no longer tolerate her lie. She confessed before the town elders that she had lied. The father of the child was not the holy monk of the desert, but the young boy next door.
>
> All of the villagers felt deeply remorseful. They immediately sought out the holy one and begged his forgiveness. They asked to have the child back. The holy one returned the child. All he said to them was, "I see. I see."

St. Paul reinforces the necessity of a humble mental attitude as he writes, "For those who live according to the flesh set their minds on the things of the flesh, but those who live according to the Spirit set their minds on the things of the Spirit. To set the mind on the flesh is death, but to set the mind on the Spirit is life and peace. For the mind that is set on the flesh is hostile to God" (Rom. 8:5–7).

One's mental attitude very much accords with one's spirituality. A living and vibrant relationship with God manifests itself in a healthy and wholesome attitude. A deep relationship with God bears the fruit of constructive and creative thinking.

Unredeemed human nature delights in various sorts of egocentric-ities. Such tendencies result in spiritual and emotional death. They set the heart opposed to God. Through and through, with a lack of yieldedness to the lordship of Jesus, pride dominates personality func-tioning.

Humility of soul, on the other hand, generates great life and peace. Herein the Holy Spirit controls the mind and fills it with all that is holy and whole. In spite of the natural tendency to dwell on the negative, the redeemed believer encounters more and more of God's work within the soul, sifting away egocentric impurities and ingraft-ing a creative and healthful interior composure.

In this state the soul experientially realizes extreme humility. Knowing that nothing proceeds out of itself, and that all comes from God within, the believer discovers great peace of soul. The inner treasure of humility richly bestows blessing after blessing in the life of such a one. God's presence experientially fills each moment of every day.

St. Basil describes this interior attentiveness to the presence of God:

> We should watch over our heart with all vigilance, not only to avoid ever losing the thought of God or sullying the memory of his wonders by vain imaginations, but also in order to carry about the holy thoughts of God stacked upon our soul as an ineffaceable seal by continuous and pure recollection . . . so the Christian directs every action, small and great, according to the will of God, performing the action at the same time with care and exactitude, and keeping his thoughts fixed upon the one who gave him the work to do. In this way he fulfills the saying, "I set the Lord always in my sights; for He is at my right hand, that I shall not be moved." And he also observed the precept, "Whether you eat or drink or whatsoever else you do, do all to the glory of God" . . . we should perform every action as if under the eyes of the Lord and think every thought as if observed by Him . . . fulfilling the words of the Lord: "I seek not my will, but the will of Him that sent me, the Father."

Dwelling constantly on the presence of Christ within unlocks vast inner treasures. Of utmost importance is the discovery of one's littleness before God. With the mind set on God in such a way, fullness of life and peace are bestowed upon the soul. God is thus experientially manifest in the soul in deeper and deeper ways.

St. Teresa of Avila wrote concerning supernatural favors and humility:

> One day whilst I was at prayer, the Lord was pleased to show me no more than His hands. Their beauty was quite beyond description. I was filled with a great fear, as usually happens when the Lord begins to grant me the experience of some supernatural favor. A few days later I also saw that divine face, and the sight seemed to transport me quite beyond myself. I could not understand why the Lord was revealing himself to me gradually in this way, for later He was to grant me the favor of seeing Him whole. Later I learned that His Majesty was making allowances for the weakness of my nature. May He be forever blessed, for so vile and base a creature as myself would not have been able to bear it, and it was because He knew this that He acted in this way.

The gradual unfolding of God's beauty sensitively regards the disposition of the human soul. We are given as much as we can endure, no more—no less. To gaze upon His face in the depths of our soul requires great yieldedness and dying to self.

Once when visiting a contemplative monastery, I was approached by one of the younger monks. He related, "I have now been in the monastery for five years. When I first arrived, I thought the silence intolerable. God's presence seemed intense, almost too intense. At times, after receiving the Eucharist, I felt overwhelmed by His purity and light. One time in particular, I feared for losing my mind. I could not fathom how the God of all purity and light could love such a creature. In the light of His presence, I seemed so dark. This experience was almost beyond my ability to endure it. As I met with my spiritual director he guided and consoled me. I no longer feel an urgency to change myself, to purify myself, to make myself more holy. Now I realize only my unworthiness, and I realize that He fully understands and loves me. My soul is at rest."

Another soul friend, Brother Patrick, a contemplative monk and cook for his community, knew God in the midst of the most mundane of daily chores. Early in the morning he would rise to prepare the

community breakfast. By midmorning he had already begun preparations for lunch. Midafternoon saw the beginnings of dinner.
Food was in the sink, boiling on the stove, and being diced on
the counter. In the midst of such routine Brother Patrick humbly
knew God.

Frequently we spoke about prayer. He confirmed that only un-
swerving attention to the presence of God yielded spiritual fruit. In
other words, the wholehearted desire and willingness to be aware of
Him predisposed the soul to communion with the Divine. Day by
day, in simple and humble ways, God blesses humble hearts.

He remarked, "Throughout the day, I strive to maintain an awareness of Him. In the midst of scrubbing pots and pans, preparing
meals, and sweeping the floor, I am with Him and He is with me."
Brother Patrick lived his days in deep prayer. Humility afforded him
the opportunity to enter into the Holy of Holies. While others in the
monastery hurried about with many "spiritual activities," Brother
Patrick met God firsthand as he engaged in the humblest of chores.
Constantly he set his mind on what the spirit desires . . . total immersion in God.

A very close associate described her encounter with God as it happened in a very unsuspected way. She traveled many, many miles to
visit a very famous monastery seeking spiritual consolation. She felt
convinced that visiting such a place of spiritual grandeur would surely
settle her restless heart. Once she arrived she initially felt relieved to
be there, only to find herself restless again after a few hours. That
which she sought was not in the grandeur of the external, but lay
within.

That night she had a dream in which she heard the words, "Leave
all and come follow me." As we talked about this dream she gradually
realized that she had been clinging to externals in an attempt to find
the kingdom within. No outer place, no external spirituality could
satisfy her interior longings. Only by humbling herself, forsaking all
save Him, would she be able to eat of the food that would forever
satisfy her.

With a humble heart, she now sought Him within her own soul. In
her words, "I need travel no more. All that I have longed for is
within me. He lives in me and I live in Him. It was both relieving
and terrifying to realize that the God of all heaven and earth dwells
within me every moment of every day. I seek now only to love Him
who dwells within me more and more deeply and completely.

Waiting on God

Waiting is the ability to be still in order to discern God's presence. Before acting on an interior inspiration, waiting must be accomplished. In other words, not every impulse and urging should be immediately taken as God's will. With patience God's presence eventually manifests itself with unshakeable surety.

One afternoon, I had finished seeing a priest for consultation. As I was walking with him down the corridor back to the reception area, I noticed that he had someone waiting for him. Another priest had evidently accompanied him in order to drive him back home.

The priest I was with introduced us. The priest who had been waiting remarked, "I know you Dr. DeBlassie." I rejoined, "Is that right?" I was unsure about what to make of his comment.

He went on, "Seventeen years ago you were leading the music for a day of renewal in a local parish. There were five or six hundred people in attendance. A nationally known speaker was praying with people after he had delivered his message. I was waiting in line for prayer. I suddenly felt the tugging interiorly to have you pray with me.

"For many years I had been struggling with a crisis in my life. I had been waiting and waiting on God. The pain that I endured grew more and more intense as time went on. That day I was seeking for God to bless me and show me the way to go.

"When I looked at you, I realized that you were only sixteen or seventeen years old. Surely the inspiration that I felt could not have come from God. The moment I tried to dismiss this thought, the more forceful it became. I finally gave in and approached you. I asked you to pray with me.

"You gently laid your hands on my head and prayed with me. What happened in the next sixty seconds changed the course of my life. It was as though my mind entered into my heart and the heavens opened up for me. I heard the voice of God, as in an inner locution. I heard His voiceless voice in a way that I had never heard before or have ever heard since. He revealed to me with utmost clarity all that I needed to know. I felt a complete assurance of God's leading and direction."

For many years this priest had been waiting on God. Finally, one day, God chose to use a rather nondescript individual to make His will known. The time of waiting, of long suffering, prepared his heart to be as yielded as possible to the transforming power of the revealed Word. From that day on he was never the same again.

I consider the plight of Gideon in the Old Testament. A person, seemingly an angel of the Lord, spoke to him and revealed that he was to bring freedom to the Israelite people. Gideon could scarcely believe what he was hearing. Before impulsively acting on this word, he waited.

The scriptures record that Gideon replied to the angel, " 'If now I have found favor with thee, then show me a sign that it is thou who speakest with me. Do not depart from here, I pray thee, until I come to thee, and bring out my present, and set it before thee.' And the Lord said, 'I will stay till you return' " (Judg. 6:17–18).

Gideon bought time. Waiting gave him the emotional distance and intellectual clarity to discern the reality of God's presence. That which is not of God eventually passes; the true presence of God grows stronger with time. Waiting helps to ensure that it is God who is really at work.

Quite often waiting produces great interior anguish and pain. Human nature seems to desire immediate gratification. When this is thwarted suffering sets in.

The enduring of such pain creates a reservoir of new grace. Rather than constantly acting on egocentered impulses the soul is steadied and made sensitive to God's movement. With this spiritual training, one is able to discern divine beckonings as opposed to egocentric inclinations.

Before being able to endure waiting, the soul frequently acts in an impulsive manner. This betrays a deeply hidden fear and insecurity. The greater the insecurity the more intense and overriding the impulsivity. Rather than facing the darkness of fear within the soul, one can choose to discharge anxiety through impulsive action. This stunts spiritual development.

When fear is brought to consciousness, in the midst of the waiting process the soul settles. Awareness of interior insecurities produces an inner equanimity. This greatly aids in enduring the time of waiting.

Everyone, to one degree or another, experiences fear during the process of waiting on God. One wonders whether God actually cares. Concerns abound over God's providence and willingness to intervene. Practically everyone seems vulnerable to such insecurity.

With the continual practice of waiting on God one learns from experience that He can be relied upon. More and more God is trusted to do what His word says He will do: "I waited patiently for the Lord; he inclined to me and heard my cry. He drew me up from the desolate pit, out of the miry bog, and set my feet upon a rock, making my steps secure. He put a new song in my mouth, a song of praise to our God. Many will see and fear, and put their trust in the Lord" (Ps. 40:1–3).

Wisdom by Fire

Wisdom is the discernment that emerges after much waiting on the presence of God. The fire of waiting cleanses the soul so that God's word is understood purely. Long suffering cultivates the ability decidedly to discern His presence.

As the story of Gideon continues, the young prophet returned to the angel with meat and a loaf of bread. The angel commanded him to place the food on top of a large rock. As we remember, Gideon was trying to discern the actual presence of God in this person. Was this or was this not an actual angel sent from Yahweh?

With the food set before him the angel placed the very tip of the staff he was carrying on the rock. Immediately fire issued forth from the staff and consumed the food. The angel immediately disappeared. The scriptures record, "Then Gideon perceived that he was the angel of the Lord; and Gideon said, 'Alas, O Lord God! For now I have seen the angel of the Lord face to face' " (Judg. 6:22). Gideon discerned the presence of God by fire.

Like Gideon, Jeremiah discerned the presence of God by fire as Yahweh declared, "Is not my word like fire, says the Lord, and like a hammer which breaks the rock in pieces?" (23:29). Isaiah confirmed this message as he proclaimed, "Behold, the name of the Lord comes from far, burning with his anger, and in thick rising smoke; his lips are full of indignation, and his tongue is like a devouring fire" (30:27).

Through an open soul God sweeps forth like a burning fire. All that is not of Him is burned away. Only His presence, His pure presence, remains in the soul. Inner, burning fire brings forth the wisdom that clearly realizes His magnificence.

One evening, as I accompanied my son to his Cub Scout meeting, I encountered a Carmelite nun I had not seen in quite a while. As we began to talk, near the entrance of the building, she caught me up on the happenings in her life. All the while, she seemed somewhat uncertain as to who I was. Finally, she candidly stated, "You sure look like Dr. Paul." I replied, "I am Dr. Paul, Sister."

Once she realized that she did indeed know me, she lit up. "I have just got to tell you about a marvelous discovery I made with your help. Last year when you conducted a healing service at our conference, I begrudgingly attended. I greatly desired to discern whether God's power really could be manifest in today's world. I just plain wanted to see for myself whether God would really heal people.

"I entered the auditorium skeptical and doubting, like doubting Thomas of old. My arms were folded and I tried to keep my mind closed. I presented every defense imaginable with regard to the super-natural workings of God. For Him to get through to me He would *really* have to get through to me.

"For a number of years I had been suffering from feelings of low self-worth. Together with this, I had experienced constant pain in my arm. Doctor after doctor could not help me either with a firm diagnosis or a treatment regimen for my arm. Nothing helped.

"As you spoke about the healing power of Jesus for our minds, our spirit, and our bodies, I sensed that God was indeed present. Soon you began to pray with people. As the prayer ministers laid hands on the hundreds of people in the auditorium, individuals began to confirm the changes that they felt physically. Those with chronic headaches no longer felt pain. Individuals suffering from backaches and neckaches felt relieved. The lame began to walk. I was stunned. For so many years I had waited, wondering if God could really come through for me. I felt confused with regard to healing. I felt confused with regard to whether God could heal me.

"When I left that day, something was changed inside of me. God touched me. Ever since that time, in God's presence, I have never been the same. I know that God loves me. I feel better about myself than I have felt in years. God healed my sense of low self-worth. I feel closer to Him and more able to love other people.

"Right after the conference I returned to my motherhouse. There I met a doctor who made a definitive diagnosis with regard to my arm. After so many years of seeking for help I finally found help when I wasn't even looking for it. A simple day surgery corrected the problem and has left me pain free. I believe that God was able to heal me, through that doctor, once He had healed me on the inside.

He took care of me on the inside, helped me to feel good on the inside, and then healed me on the outside."

After many years of waiting, this Carmelite nun's confusion subsided. She came upon wisdom by fire. In her words, "During the healing service, when I witnessed God's healing presence firsthand, I felt the fire of His love from the top of my head to the tips of my toes. The fire of God burned through and through." With patient waiting on God, wisdom emerges . . . by fire.

Spirituality

Jesus declared, " 'Woman, believe me, the hour is coming when neither on this mountain nor in Jerusalem will you worship the Father. You worship what you do not know; we worship what we know, for salvation is from the Jews. But the hour is coming, and now is, when the true worshipers will worship the Father in spirit and truth, for such the Father seeks to worship him. God is spirit, and those who worship him must worship in spirit and truth' " (John 4:21–24).

The inner treasure of spirituality is discovered when one comes to "know" Jesus. A heart-to-heart encounter with the living presence of Jesus within the soul is the hallmark of true spirituality. At such moments the Father reveals the presence of Jesus in spirit. The mind then comprehends the reality of His lordship and is transformed.

I frequently witness many people, young people especially, seeking various forms of spiritual experiences. They may leave their Christian roots in order to search for "truth." Their hunger and thirst is to find that which satisfies. I respect their need for such a quest.

In the end, however, only an encounter with Jesus as Lord satisfies this human longing. He is the all in all. No other experience with any other proffered spirituality can fill the yearnings of the human heart.

During the late sixties and early seventies, the Jesus movement swept through this country. During this time I remember young people saying that they were "high on God." I knew what they meant. I was high on God. I am high on God.

In the words of one young college student, "I have always heard about Jesus. I attended Catholic grade school. I went to Mass every Sunday with my family. Jesus, Jesus, Jesus . . . that's all I ever heard.

But, who was this Jesus? I heard about Him. I learned a lot about Him. I never knew Him. He could have a radical effect on my life only if I somehow could feel the power of His presence.

"One day somebody asked me if I felt empty on the inside. Of course, I responded that I indeed felt incredibly empty. He told me about his experience with Jesus. One day after feeling as lost and confused as ever he opened his heart sincerely and prayed. He spoke directly to Jesus, person to person. He spoke to Jesus from his soul. He asked Jesus to come into his life, to change his heart and live in him forever. At that very moment God communicated Himself to him spirit to spirit.

"That's just what I did. Right there in the middle of the university campus we found a quiet place to pray together. This guy required no formal doctrinal pledges or other commitments on my part. He just wanted to share with me the God who had changed his life. With all of my heart I prayed and opened myself up. I felt His presence come in to me. That's the best way I can explain it.

"I sensed Jesus on the inside of me. Just like I can see you and feel that you are here with me, that's just how I felt Jesus. In fact, when I close my eyes and become quiet I can feel Him on the inside of me, all of the time. When I stood up from that prayer I felt high on God."

Deep prayer caused a spiritual revolution in this young man's life. In that moment in which he was open to God wholeheartedly, God made Himself known to him. He found the inner treasure of spirituality when he found a living relationship with Jesus.

The inner experience of the Holy brings an individual to the knowledge that God resides within, not without. Because of this, people, institutions, or movements no longer carry the projection of the Holy. That is to say, enslaving identification with such entities is no longer a necessity, since personal growth has propelled one to dynamic interior change and personal responsibility for spirituality.

Without the personal knowledge of God, institutions and groups of various sorts often carry the responsibility of holiness for the individual. In these cases, one looks to leaders within such groups as spiritual idols. In traditional Christianity ministers or priests may even carry the full weight of responsibility for the spirituality of a given people. An individual need not assume personal responsibility for Christian advancement when a designated church authority is posed as the special man or woman of spirituality. Priests and ministers may be regarded with such awe that they become a type of god for the person. Rather than following the inner leadings of the Holy Spirit, people can look to these religious leaders and follow them blindly. Of necessity this dwarfs spiritual development.

With the living experience of Jesus Christ in the heart, the individual now moves into a zealous relationship with God. External supports, such as religious institutions and ecclesiastical authorities, may support and nourish the interior development but in no way supplant it. The pure essence of God is communicated spirit to spirit. Authentic spirituality has arisen in such a soul.

Without a living relationship with God in the depths of the soul problems with religious practice abound. The institutions or clergy that are regarded with godlike awe are eventually bound to reveal human limitations and even failings. When this dawns on the follower, great scandal and disbelief flood the mind. Projections of perfection and otherworldly holiness come tumbling down, painfully. Quite often, this only causes the follower to seek after another "perfect church" or "a more godlike or spiritual pastor." Thus, the projection of personal spiritual responsibility worsens and worsens.

The only relief possible comes from finally realizing, in truth, the human condition. No one is perfect, no institution or religious body is without fault. No one can assume spiritual responsibility for you. God is spirit and you must know him in your spirit. No one else can do this for you. True spirituality, in the end, is a matter between you and God . . . God deeply committed to you and you deeply committed to God.

Obedience: Following Jesus

Just as the inner treasure of spirituality refers to knowing Jesus, so the inner treasure of obedience means to follow Jesus. The silent whispering of God's voice in the soul calls for obedience. As we follow Him, spirituality enlivens the soul.

Indeed, Jesus declared, " 'My food is to do the will of him who sent me, and to accomplish his work" (John 4:34). Jesus regarded accomplishing the will of the Father as interior food. It nourished and sustained Him. Unreservedly following God's will truly satisfies all interior cravings.

Mature obedience does not require blind faith. Instead, the individual remains highly conscious and willfully cooperative. Without the feeling of responding to God consciously and wholeheartedly, one can become crippled emotionally and spiritually. That is to say, freely responding to God, out of the conscious awareness of His calling, cultivates interior development.

The community may assist the individual to arrive at a clear discernment, but it can in no way replace one's clearminded discernment and response to the Divine. When group pressure overrules God's intimate guidance in the individual's soul, spiritual poverty may result. Abundance in life consists only in following Him, not in acquiescence to collective demands.

Intense group pressure often signals the uprising of collective egocentricity. God's guidings are firm and gentle without being anxiety-producing. Once a tormenting tension develops with regard to others' opinions, one can rest assured that a highly egocentric power motivates the group. In opposition to this the believer must stand.

St. Augustine magnificently describes the revelation of the word of God to the human heart:

This then, Oh God, was the Beginning in which you created Heaven and Earth: marvelously speaking and marvelously creating in Your Word. Who is Your Son and Your Strength and Your Wisdom, and Your Truth! Who shall understand this? Who shall relate it? What is that light which shines upon me, but not continuously, and strikes upon my heart with no wounding? I draw back in terror: I am on fire with longing: terror is so far as I am different from it, longing in the degree of my likeness to it. It is Wisdom, Wisdom itself, which in these moments shines upon me, cleaving through my cloud. And the cloud returns to wrap me round once more as my strength is beaten down under its darkness and the weight of my sins: for my strength is weakened through poverty, so that I can no longer support my good, until thou, Lord, who are merciful to my iniquities, shalt likewise heal my weakness: redeeming my life from corruption and crowning me with pity and compassion, and filling my desire with good things: my youth shall be renewed like the eagle's. For we are saved by hope and we wait with patience for Thy promises.

Let him who can hear Thy voice speaking within Him; I, relying upon Thy inspired word, shall cry aloud: How great are Thy words, oh Lord! Thou hast made all things in wisdom. Wisdom is "the beginning": In that Beginning, that you made heaven and earth.

Continual following of Jesus requires an inner attentiveness. He leads first from within and then prompts outward actions. His inner workings in the soul always take precedence over outer guidance with regard to our life circumstances. He is first and foremost a God of the kingdom within.

In the words of St. Theopan the Recluse,

> The spiritual world is open to him who lives within himself. By remaining within and gazing upon this vision of the other world, we arouse a sense of warmth in our spiritual feelings: and conversely, the same sense of spiritual warmth enables us to dwell within, and awakens our awareness of the inner spiritual realm. The spiritual life matures by the mutual action of both these things—inwardness and warmth. He who lives in spiritual feeling and warmth of heart has his spirit bound and tied, but the spirit of the man who lacks this warmth will wander. Therefore, so as to further constant inwardness, strive after warmth of heart; but strive, also, through intense effort, to enter and remain within. That is why he who seeks to remain collected only in the mind—without warmth of heart—strives in vain: in a moment everything is dispersed. And so it is no wonder that, in spite of all their education, scientists constantly miss the truth—it is because they work only with their head.

Following Jesus from the heart summarizes the Christian vocation. Nothing more is required. Diligently to seek after Him, hearing His voice within, leads one to an ever-deepening encounter with the risen Jesus. The inner treasure of obedience kindles the fire of warm love for a loving Savior.

Inspiration

Inspiration is the spirit of God breathed into the soul. The Divine Presence communicates itself to the soul via inspiration. His breath breathed into our soul enlivens and freshens the most weary spiritual traveler. The sacred scriptures record the very first moment of divine inspiration: "Then the Lord God formed man of dust from the ground, and breathed into his nostrils the breath of life; and man became a living being" (Gen. 2:7).

In reflecting on the experience of inspiration, St. Paul in his letter to the Colossians helps to provide fuller understanding: "That their hearts may be encouraged as they are knit together in love, to have all the riches of assured understanding and the knowledge of God's mystery, of Christ, in whom are hid all the treasures of wisdom and knowledge" (2:2–3).

Christ, the mystery of God, God's own inspiration, has hidden within Him treasures of wisdom and knowledge. Inspiration produces a keenness of knowledge and wisdom. Spiritual knowledge refers to knowledge of Christ. St. Paul declares, in his letter to the Philippians, "That I may know him and the power of resurrection, and may share his sufferings, becoming like him in his death, that if possible I may attain the resurrection from the dead" (3:10–11). Inspiration ushers the knowledge of Christ into the soul with piercing clarity.

A young man candidly disclosed to me his cross of many years and the consequent light and knowledge he came to realize as the result of enduring this pain. Over a period of three years, he had experienced the death of four family members. This left him devastated and grief-filled. In an attempt to find consolation and relief he sought spiritual direction.

Under the guidance of a spiritual director, trained in depth psychology, he plummeted into the depths of his soul. For many months he waded through the darkness of grief and tragedy, feelings that plagued his painridden heart. He thought that his ordeal would be never ending.

Finally, many months later, he had the following dream: "I was walking down a very winding and steep mountainous path. My spiritual director was by my side. after an incredibly long period of time, or so it seemed, we reached an open meadow. We still had a ways to go, but the majority of the journey had been completed. I looked up to the sky, admiring the blueness and brightness of the horizon, when all of a sudden a beautiful white bird approached me. It sang a song of unearthly beauty. The song resonated within me. It was my song. When I awakened, I realized that God had placed a new song in my heart. Where deeply held grief and sadness once crippled my innermost being, I now sang a new song. In no way was my spiritual journey completed, but I had experienced a very definite transformation within."

This man realized a greater knowledge of the presence of Jesus within. Jesus emerged within him as a new song in his heart. From the depths of his unconscious, inspiration and knowledge issued forth. He felt closer to God as old feelings of grief were worked through. In the words of the psalmist, "He put a new song in my mouth, a song of praise to our God. Many will see and fear, and put their trust in the Lord" (40:3).

Along with knowledge, wisdom saturates the soul of one divinely inspired. Wisdom is clarity of mind and surety of heart. It helps one to realize what to do in a given situation. With wisdom the believer clearly perceives the will of God.

"Behold, thou desirest truth in the inward being; therefore teach me wisdom in my secret heart" (ps. 51:6). The inner self is the repository of all wisdom. God's will, past, present, and future, resides deeply in the self.

For this reason when the soul opens itself to God during moments of deep prayer wisdom comes forth. A keen awareness of God's presence inspires the soul with clarity of discernment. God reveals all wisdom to one who honestly seeks for Him within.

A very distraught middle-aged minister approached me one evening after a seminar. He remarked, "Dr. DeBlassie, I know the importance of seeking God from the depths of my being. Not too long ago I felt great conflict over two courses of action. One way would definitely please my congregation. The other way I knew was God's way. My congregation would not understand my needing to follow God in the manner I discerned. I would be shunned and possible even fired. My conflict raged within me.

"Night after night I wrestled with God. Finally one evening a dream came. In the dream I was rushed to the emergency room of a local hospital. There the doctor told me that I had a choice. In order to treat my pain I could either have an adulterous relationship or submit to surgery. As with most dreams the situation seemed irrational. But underlying this ridiculous predicament in my dreams was great truth.

"In a split second I knew that I had to submit to surgery. Even though it would be painful, it was what I had to do. Once I spoke with my spiritual director I realized the full implication of this dream. Having an adulterous relationship would be like making the decision to be a people-pleaser. This would be a betrayal of my very soul. I would turn my face away from Jesus in doing this. On the other hand, I could submit to God's will, even though it would be very painful, much like surgery. I would have to die to my own selfish ways and submit to God. This was the way for me.

"The dream ended with me sitting in a large room filled with holy people. We were listening to an old woman describe the glories of

God. I could enter this room only if I had chosen to have the surgery. I had chosen to undergo surgery, had completed my surgery, and was therefore allowed into the room. In the room, as the woman spoke, God's presence illumined everyone. I felt the awe of knowing Him."

In a time of great desperation God inspired this minister with wisdom. Through his dream he found clarity of mind and surety of heart to follow the will of God. In so doing he encountered God's glory within his soul in a new and vibrant dimension. He encountered Jesus, the very wisdom of God. "He is the source of your life in Christ Jesus, whom God made our wisdom, our righteousness and sanctification and redemption" (1 Cor. 1:30).

Littleness

Littleness, a profound revelation of wisdom, is an inner treasure of incomparable delight. Jesus becomes our everything, and all actions proceed out of an immersion in the awareness of His presence. St. Thérèse, the Little Flower, described the little way of spiritual childhood as an unshakeable confidence in God's love with complete understanding that what mattered most in life is, "not great deeds but great love."

This saying captures the beauty of the inner treasure of littleness. According to the egocentric ego greatness is perpetually striven after. Jesus, however, beckons the believer to littleness. In Him all that is exalted will be humbled and all that is little shines forth with His glory.

The saints of old all discovered the inner treasure of littleness. It is reputed that St. Francis of Assisi and St. Ignatius of Loyola both exchanged their own garments with filthy beggars. Saints such as Francis of Assisi and others purposely sought interior littleness as the most supreme path to God.

Pascal amply expressed his own self-surrender and littleness:

Deliver me, Lord, from the sadness at my proper suffering which self-love might give, but put into me a sadness like your own. Let my sufferings appease your choler, make them an occasion for my conversion and salvation. I ask you neither for help nor for sickness, for life nor for death; but that you may dispose of my health and my sickness, my life and my death, for your glory, for my salvation, and for the use of the

Church and of your saints, of whom I would by your grace be one. You alone know what is expedient for me; you are the Sovereign Master; do with me according to your will. Give to me, or take away from me, only to conform my will to yours. I know but one thing, Lord, that it is good to follow you, and bad to offend you. Apart from that, I know not what is good or bad in anything. I know not which is most profitable to me, health or sickness, wealth or poverty, nor anything else in the world. That discernment is beyond the power of man or angels, and is hidden among the secrets of your Providence, which I adore, but do not seek to fathom.

Anthony, a fifty-three-year-old committed Catholic, confided in me one evening, "I feel so empty and almost desperate on the inside. At church everyone avoids me. I know that I have a lot to give, but somehow it just does not come through."

He spoke in a rather stilted and hesitating manner. Emotionally he seemed very flat and highly reserved. I could tell that he felt a great deal of interior pain and anguish. He needed help.

As he and I talked together in a private area, away from the other retreatants, the source of his agony became apparent. The night before he had the following dream: He found himself in a very old church speaking with an old priest friend. It was time to say goodbye. With great reluctance he was leaving the church, his youth, and the older priest who had befriended him for many years. As he looked around the church it felt empty. The old priest, a very arrogant and indolent fellow, also knew that their friendship was over. The dream ended.

As we discussed this dream Anthony suddenly realized that he had felt a change coming on in his life. Old ways of relating to people and to former spiritual practices no longer felt right. He had lived in a very superficial and detached manner when it came to dealing with others. He rarely shared intimately with anyone. This obviously left him feeling very alone and isolated.

Spiritually, he had been accustomed to what might be referred to as the external forms of religion. He had greatly enjoyed elaborate and complicated religious rituals. Adornments and pomp at one time inspired him with religious fervor. Now . . . all of that left him high and dry.

The old priest represented an arrogance of soul. Deep within his own unconscious he regarded others as inferior to himself. This betrayed his own personal sense of inadequacy. When one feels good about himself or herself others are always related to as equals with respect and understanding. He had always related in a condescending manner. The time had now come to leave this behind.

The way of littleness began to emerge before him. He looked at me with great relief and intense perplexity. He did not know what the future would hold for him. He understood only that spiritual and emotional arrogance had been healed within him, signaling the dawning of a new relationship with those whom he loved and with the God that he longed to be closer to each moment of every day. All of his questions had not been answered in our conversation, but one thing he did know: littleness of soul generates blessings. Anthony left that evening feeling greatly relieved, greatly blessed, and enormously challenged.

I am reminded of the story of the little turtle. As it goes, the emperor of China was searching all over his kingdom to find a suitable prime minister. After having interviewed scores and scores of men, he finally heard about a wise and holy man who greatly helped those who sought his counsel. He immediately decided that this hermit would be suitable to fill the role of prime minister. The emperor sent his most esteemed general to invite the hermit to become prime minister of China.

The emperor and his cohort eventually discovered the hermit fishing in the middle of a very muddy river. He looked to be of such low demeanor that they wondered whether this could actually be the fellow they were seeking. The local townspeople confirmed that indeed this was the holy man. So the general very respectfully approached the hermit.

"Holy one," the general began, "I come as a messenger of his lordship, the emperor. Having heard of your great wisdom and holiness, the emperor invites you to accept the post of the most distinguished prime minister of the kingdom."

"Me?" the holy man questioned. "Yes, you," the general responded. "Is the emperor out of his mind?" roared the holy man with great and exuberant laughter.

With great uneasiness the general asked, "Why would you not want to accept such a dignified post?" The holy man replied, "Dear sir, is it true that the emperor's home has a great altar in the chapel and on top of this altar is a stuffed turtle encrusted with sparkling diamonds?" "Yes, this is true," replied the general. "And is it true that every day the emperor and his household gather together to worship this stuffed and diamond-decorated turtle?" "Yes, it is true," replied the general.

The holy man then pointed to a little turtle sitting gaily on a rock near the river. The holy man asked the general, "Do you think that this lowly creature here would dare to change places with the turtle in the emperor's chapel?" The general immediately replied, "No, of course not."

The holy man then rejoined, "Then go tell the emperor that neither would I. No one who is placed on a pedestal can be really alive."

In the words of St. Teresa of Avila, "We shall never succeed in knowing ourselves unless we seek to know God. By looking at His greatness, we become aware of our own vileness; by looking on His purity, we see our own impurity; by considering His humility, we see how far we are from being humble."

The call to littleness is an eternal call. From the beginning of time God created us to decrease so that He might increase. In this we discover exhilarating fulfillment.

With the awareness of personal nothingness things work together for the good. God is set free to work in the soul that realizes that egocentric strivings result in nothing but futility. With Him, however, all things are brought to completion and resolution.

Linda, a woman with a vivaciously free spirit, painfully learned the importance of littleness. Years of loneliness plagued and haunted her. To others she appeared uppity and somewhat condescending. Yet she seemed to have a very latent potential to feel for others. To her great dismay others seemed never to find time for her and related to her in a very superficial manner.

After having addressed her women's Bible study group, I opened up the discussion for questions. She immediately raised her hand and asked whether God indeed speaks to human beings, in this day and age, through dreams. I explained to her the biblical precedent for God's will being communicated through dreams, then assured her that God spoke today to men and women through this means. After the presentation, she privately shared with me a very impactful dream.

The night before the Bible study meeting she dreamed that she was building bridges. Bridge after bridge she would build, never feeling tired or exasperated. In fact, with each new endeavor, she felt strengthened. She awakened feeling energized.

As we discussed the meaning of this dream she understood that she had recently begun feeling a new impetus to reach out to others. Rather than remaining such an uppity and "above-it-all" sort of person, she felt a new kinship with friends and acquaintances. In her words, "I guess I have been a little condescending with others. I always expected other people to come to me. I never wanted to do the calling or the visiting. I figured that if they really wanted to get to know me, they should just go out of their way and do it. I would never reach out. It's time for me to start building bridges."

Such insightfulness renders the soul available to the inner treasure of littleness. Instead of being caught in vicious cycles that perpetuate needless pain and loneliness, personal growth can be fostered through depth of understanding. The soul requires great littleness to experience great blessings.

Thomas Merton richly describes the experience of the inner treasure of littleness as he writes, "I have only one desire . . . to disappear into God, to be submerged in His peace, to be lost in the secret of His face."

Strength

Interior strength emerges within the individual once identification with personal power has been obliterated. In the words of the epistle to the Corinthians, " 'My grace is sufficient for you, for my power is made perfect in weakness" (2 Cor. 12:9). God's power at work in the soul arises out of times of seeming doubt, insecurity, and anxiety. His power is at work within you when you least suspect it.

As strength of soul is born it can be depended upon, for it is God's own strength, rather than egocentered and selfish power at work. Confidently and assuredly one must move forward with this new insight. Strength empowers one to live boldly and creatively in spite of periodic and passing whispering doubts.

Helen Luke in *The Voice Within* notes, "There is a 'Wormtongue' in all of us, whispering doubt as to our strength, counseling prudence and compromise in all the wrong places, telling us that we are too weak to make clear decisions that may prove mistaken, or to take up this or that responsibility, that we cannot draw the sword or stand firm—for all sorts of speciously sensible reasons."

A young Catholic nun felt deeply distressed regarding her inability to allow herself to be strong. Time and time again, her superiors commented on her unnatural docility and passivity. "They used to tell me, 'You just don't express yourself. We are worried about you. It's like you are afraid to speak your mind. On important matters and even unimportant matters you withhold your view and acquiesce to the group. Something just feels too unnatural about all of this.' "

The "sweet and nice" religious sister could hardly remember ever feeling upset or angry. In fact, she prided herself in never allowing negative emotions like anger and fear to step into her awareness. Surely, she thought, this was the ultimate in sanctity. Her spiritual director and religious superiors, however, did not agree with her. Something felt all too unnatural about her "perfect" behavior.

Sister Dorothy, this ostensibly meek and mild nun, respected the concern of her superiors. She decided to seek God regarding the matter. One afternoon in the convent chapel, after an hour of prayer, the image of her father with her older brother came in to her mind in a most terrifying manner. She recalled, indeed relived, an incident of horrible family violence that occurred when she was approximately eight years of age.

In the family den her father whipped and beat her brother until he was bleeding. Her brother was then approximately fifteen years of age. All control and discretion were lost to her father during this time. He chased his son throughout the house, beating him and beating him. Yelling and screaming, blood and tears plagued this pain-filled hour. Finally, her father collapsed from exhaustion. She remembered thinking, "I will never be angry. I will never lose control. I will never be strong because I could hurt someone like my father has hurt my brother."

Alone in the chapel, pain swept through her soul. She wanted to flee from prayer. She realized that there was no escaping this inner torment. It needed to be faced and understood. She sat with her pain in the presence of God for another two hours. This crucifixion exhausted her.

Later that evening, as she lay on her bed in the still of night, a clear understanding of her unfeeling meekness filled her mind. She recounted to me, "To be strong meant to be like my father. I never wanted to hurt anyone the way that he hurt my brother. I withheld all of my anger, all of my strength, all of my feelings so as not to be like my father. I achieved my goal. In no way was I like my father:

but in so doing, I lost hold of my own soul. For the next few hours I knelt beside my bed acutely aware of God's presence. I felt pain and I felt healing.

"I knew that if I could endure this agony I would have made a decisive step toward my healing. For the next few hours I remained with Him. I felt that I too was on the cross with my distress and anguish. There was no way off this cross. I had to go through with it.

"Sometimes you've just got to hang on the cross. There is no way down. You've just got to hang there. At the end of my prayer I didn't feel better. I felt stronger."

Inner treasures are discovered through moments of deep prayer. Humility, waiting, wisdom, spirituality, obedience, inspirations, littleness, and strength all radiantly reflect, as magnificent gems, the splendor of the kingdom within. St. Francis of Rome imparted this intimate perception of the divine love during deep prayer:

I saw a very dazzling light that hovered over a dense darkness. Within this light there was a tabernacle full of splendor, and above this tabernacle was our Savior in His sacred human form, and His holy wounds streamed forth rays that garmented the saints with wonderful glory.

5

God's Presence Is in the Everlasting Now

"And lo, I am with you always, to the close of the age" (Matt. 28:20).

Jesus promised His guiding presence as a surety in every life situation. He is not with you sometimes and at other times not. His presence pervades all that we do, think, aspire, and suffer. Through thick and thin, He lives with you.

Eternity flows with each moment. His everlasting presence takes hold in each everlasting now. Longing for future blessings dilutes God's manifestation in the present. It interrupts a wholehearted yieldedness to Him in the moment under the guise of trusting Him for the future. Embracing God fully at this very moment with eager expectation of grace upon grace opens the floodgates of heaven.

Jesus, and only Jesus, provides this surety of bountiful living. Only He moves with such depth and breadth interiorly that past and future are providentially taken care of, rejuvenated, and anticipated by living fully with Him in the present moment. The past and future take care of themselves as Jesus Christ, not the personal ego, reigns supreme in the moment.

Anger Is Pure and Holy

Since God is a now God, he meets every practical and daily need. In joys and sorrows, His grace abounds. In love and anger He is there. Purity and holiness exude from the full range of human experience and emotion. Purity and holiness are imbedded even in anger.

Anger is love made hungry. An individual tormented with chronic anger needs to understand the purpose and place of this intense emotion. Somewhere inside, the need for love has been frustrated and unfulfilled. Cravings for love left unsatisfied eventually turn into anger and rage. Criticism, rejection, and abandonment generate anger because the soul has not felt loved. Thus, an angry soul is a love-starved soul.

The psalmist vividly describes loveless and attacking encounters with people:

> If it had not been the Lord who was on our side, let Israel now say—if it had not been the Lord who was on our side, when men rose up against us, then they would have swallowed us up alive, when their anger was kindled against us; then the flood would have swept us away, the torrent would have gone over us; then over us would have gone the raging waters. Blessed be the Lord, who has not given us as prey to their teeth! We have escaped as a bird from the snare of the fowlers; the snare is broken, and we have escaped! Our help is in the name of the Lord, who made heaven and earth. (Ps. 124)

Tom, a fifty-two-year-old university professor, noticed himself feeling inexplicably irritable and tired. A feeling of being out of sorts crept over his sense of emotional well-being. Even though he practiced prayer daily, using the Jesus Prayer, the uneasy feeling persisted. For two days this emotional affliction gnawed away at him.

Finally, on a Wednesday afternoon at approximately 5:30 in the evening, he had finished his time of meditation with the Jesus Prayer. As He slowly opened his eyes and sat comfortably in his chair, the thought of his wife crossed his mind. He recalled that three days before she had left on a business trip. Before her departure, they had quarreled, leaving Tom with the feeling of being misunderstood. In fact, he realized that somewhere on the inside he wondered whether she really loved him. Rationally, of course, he knew that she deeply cared for him and very much loved him, but his emotions were not rational.

He came to understand that his feelings of being ill at ease were in actuality feelings of anger. Without having resolved their argument, he felt a lack of love from his wife. The unconscious always interprets a lack of understanding as a lack of love. When a person does not feel understood, he or she does not feel loved. Tom felt the deep pain and anger of not feeling loved.

As he reflected on the truth about what happened between him and his wife, an emotional settledness took hold of him. Tom recalled, "The matter had not been rectified since my wife was still out of town, but I felt better and more at ease knowing that I was angry because I, in some irrational way, questioned her love for me. I now knew that once she came back into town we would talk things over and come to an understanding. I looked forward to seeing her on Friday."

When she returned from her business trip on Friday she and Tom went to dinner. After a relaxing meal, Tom brought up his concern. They were able to talk together in a respectful and open manner. After a great deal of heart-to-heart sharing, they both felt understood by each other. They both felt loved. As depth of understanding becomes actualized in human relationships, anger ceases. Anger is always a cry for love.

Deep prayer, as experienced through the use of the Jesus Prayer, helped Tom to quiet his soul and find the inspiration that eventually brought him to healing. Quietness and calm soothe the most anger-torn soul. The comfort of prayer readies the soul to experience the love of God and the love of others. Divine peacefulness felt in and through deep prayer surfaces the holiness and purity of God's own presence within anger. The intense emotion of anger is merely a shell that encases a love-hungry heart longing to be set free to love.

In the words of the psalmist,

> Out of my distress I called on the Lord; the Lord answered me and set me free. . . . Thou art my God, and I will give thanks to thee; thou art my God, I will extol thee. O give thanks to the Lord, for he is good; for his steadfast love endures for ever! (Ps. 118:5, 28–29)

Guilt—A Giver of Grace

Guilt is anger turned against the self. Anger directed inward causes feelings of self-condemnation and self-reproach. Negative thoughts plague the mind. Pessimism with regard to the past, present, and future occupy one's outlook.

Intense and chronic guilt causes ailments ranging from mild to severe depression and a whole host of physical difficulties. Unresolved guilt is self-destructive mentally, spiritually, and physically. An individual can literally be set on a sure course toward self-destruction by leaving guilt feelings unresolved.

Through the realization that guilt is anger turned against the self, the believer has the opportunity to encounter God in and through guilt. In this manner guilt becomes a giver of grace. In actuality, God is encountered in and through feelings of guilt as healing takes place. The underlying cause of guilt—anger turned against the self—is surrendered into the arms of a loving Father. Slowly, over time, relief can fill the soul.

A young religious sister confided: "I was raised in a family that preached the wrath and judgment of God. Both of my parents were very angry people. I grew up believing that I needed to stay by God for fear of eternal damnation. Guilt prompted my every religious action.

"Once I entered my religious order, unfortunately, this mentality was even more ingrained into my mind and soul. Once, for a very minor infraction of talking at a time of silence during retreat, I was required to scrub the hallway floor with a toothbrush as penance. This took me a total of three solid working days, twenty-four work hours to be exact. My knees were sore, my back ached, and I felt like a miserable peon.

"I felt so plagued by a guilt-ridden conscience that I, at one point, could not go to confession in a chapel where the blessed sacrament was exposed. I felt too unworthy. I caught the priest outside in the parking lot right before he drove away. I begged him to hear my confession in his car. I could not bear the thought of such a wretched creature as myself entering a room where the blessed sacrament was present.

"Fortunately, my spiritual director urged me to consider psychotherapy. I found that it facilitated my spiritual growth and unearthed deeply buried feelings of unresolved guilt. After a year and a half in psychotherapy, I felt freer and closer to God than ever before in my life. The less condemnation that I had on the inside of me, the more I felt God on the inside of me."

Through painstaking soul-searching, the Catholic nun discovered that guilt is a giver of grace. Guilt signals that anger is at work in a destructive manner. It sounds an alarm that healing is needed. A deep understanding of the meaning of guilt serves to liberate the soul with the very grace of God.

St. Paul firmly declares, "There is therefore now no condemnation for those who are in Christ Jesus. For the law of the Spirit of life in Christ Jesus has set me free from the law of sin and death" (Rom.

8:1–2). The gospel message flows with grace, triumphing over condemnation. Spiritual death ensues with self-condemnation. Life results from God's forgiveness and self-forgiveness.

After a recent session at a local youth conference, a young teenager told me, "I know the feeling of condemnation. I want to live my life for God, but at times I give in to my old ways. At a college party last weekend, I had too much to drink and really felt horrible. I felt far away from God. I began to get down on myself. I was so hard on myself that I literally felt drained and worthless. This is self-condemnation. I was dead on the inside.

"Today, after hearing your message, I realize that condemnation means despairing over past mistakes. God forgives my mistakes. The trouble is that sometimes I don't forgive myself for my mistakes. This is when despair sets in. This is condemnation, self-condemnation. Realizing this has set me free. I'm the one who does the condemning of myself. God is the one who wants to do the forgiving. I think that from now on I'm going to side with God. No more condemnation for me. I feel alive with God on the inside of me now."

Fear—Frozen Love

Deeply understanding God's life at work in the soul liberates one from destructive anger, badgering guilt, and paralyzing fear. One of the most powerful realizations that removes the yoke of fear is that God is a day-by-day God. Realizing the distinction between a once-and-for-all God and a day-by-day God holds the potential to loosen the shackles of personal fear and terrors.

Believing that God requires and expects everything to be perfect in your life right now sets up a condition bound for failure. Imperfection characterizes all of humanity. God understands our shortcomings, faults, and limitations. In fact, He calls us to glorify Him in them rather than to decry them. A personal problem signals an opportunity to trust God more than ever before, day by day.

To anticipate that one of these days life will suddenly change and be pain-free and problem-free, once and for all, departs from the Christian message and riddles the soul with fear. It fixes our gaze upon outer circumstances rather than on the inner Jesus. Egocentricities and fears nestle into the soul that is no longer wholeheartedly focused on Jesus. With unwavering conviction regarding God's faithfulness, problems and even crises provide no cause for alarm or despair. Trusting in Him day by day means maintaining a firm faith that He is at work in the everlasting now. He is the ultimate transformer of fear into faith.

The second letter to the Corinthians eloquently describes the inward journey from fear to faith: "So we do not lose heart. Though our outer nature is wasting away, our inner nature is being renewed every day. For this slight momentary affliction is preparing for us an eternal weight of glory beyond all comparison, because we look not to the things that are seen but to the things that are unseen; for the things that are seen are transient, but the things that are unseen are eternal" (4:16–18).

A fear-ridden person has lost heart. That is to say, a person troubled by fear manifests little or no emotional warmth, seems withdrawn, and in general appears quite frozen. Frozen feelings characterize a heart depressed by fear. St. Paul urges Christians, " . . . do not lose heart." In other words, it is all too easy to allow fear to dominate the personality. In such cases a deep sense of emotional bondage and oppression plagues the soul. Rather than being inwardly renewed day by day, outer and inner troubles cramp the soul like massive burdens thwarting spiritual growth. Contact with the loving God and with loving humans has been lost.

Dr. Harry Guntrip, an English depth psychologist, wrote, "You cannot easily get in touch with the heart of the fear-ridden person, due to a seeming lack of ability to show emotional warmth and liveliness. The living heart of him has fled from the scene, has regressed deep within, and he has lost the true self without which he cannot form loving ties."

At times fear expresses itself in an oppositional manner. Barbara, a woman in her late thirties, approached me one evening after a conference. She very enthusiastically shared, "I know exactly what you mean when you speak of the fear-ridden person. I had been plagued by fear for the great majority of my life. However, rather than withdrawing, I came across like a bull in a china closet.

"Whenever I was shaking with fear on the inside I would overreact on the outside. I would come across strong, too strong. This made me feel powerful for a little while. Because I was so overbearing I was seen as intrusive and insensitive. Others shied away from me.

"No one ever really ever knew me. You see, the real me was hidden way down deep inside. I had experienced so much rejection in my life that I just decided I would never be rejected again. In fact, I would be the one to do the rejecting. I became a master of emotional abuse and assault. It protected me from facing my fear.

"Finally, I decided to enter psychotherapy. My pastor encouraged me to consider it. After about six months I really felt like I was beginning to deal with my hidden-away fears. You would think that other Christians would have supported me during this healing time. Some did and some didn't.

"One person, who I thought was a friend of mine, told me quite brutally, 'I don't know why you are in psychotherapy. Jesus is my healer. He is all that I need.' I turned to her and very directly said, 'Jesus is my healer too. He is healing me through deep counseling.'

"Now after about a year and a half of counseling I am finally feeling like I am becoming the person that God created me to be. I am not afraid to feel anymore. It even feels good to be angry, to grieve, to experience joy, really to feel love. It's a whole new world for me now."

As I looked at her I sensed the presence of a real person. The real Barbara was speaking with me. Her feelings were warm and genuine. I sensed that now, with the thawing of her emotions, she lived life to the fullest. I believe Barbara experientially understood that "inwardly we are being renewed day by day."

Frozen love, fear, can plague even one's daily relationship with God. Father Thomas, a priest for over twenty years, confided that he had never truly allowed himself to experience God. He maintained a very reserved and controlled spirituality. His relationship with God was both stiff and dry.

Finally, after admitting to a chronic problem with alcohol, he surrendered his life fully to God. For the first time in his life, he yielded his whole soul to his Creator. A near-death calamity, due to his excessive drinking, literally brought him to his knees before God. Prior to this he had maintained the external forms of religion. By all outward signs he was considered quite pious and religious. He knew better. Fear of God motivated his religiosity and prompted his alcoholism.

While lying in a detoxification unit at an inpatient alcoholism treatment center, he cried out to God for mercy and love. Soon after his prayer, he felt an indescribable interior peace. Much to his surprise he encountered not a judging deity but a loving Father. For years to come he remembered that moment with great tenderness and conviction. His heart, once frozen by fear, now stirred with the warmth of the love of God.

Anthony de Mello, in his book *The Song of the Bird,* records a short narrative entitled "The Look of Jesus":

> In the Gospel according to Luke we read: But Peter said, "Man, I do not know what you are talking about." At that moment, while he was still speaking, a cock crew; and the Lord turned and looked straight at Peter . . . and Peter went outside and wept bitterly. I had a fairly good relationship with the Lord. I would ask Him for things, converse with Him, praise Him, thank Him. . . . But always I had this uncomfortable feeling that He wanted me to look at Him. And I would not. I would talk, but look away when I sensed that He was looking at me. I was afraid. I should find an accusation there of some unrepented sin. I thought I should find a demand there; there would be something He wanted from me.
>
> One day I finally summed up courage and looked! There was no accusation. There was no demand. The eyes just said, "I love you."
>
> And I walked out and, like Peter, I wept.

Dreams: God's Forgotten Language

"I slept, but my heart was awake" (Song of Sol. 5:2). During sleep, the heart of the believer remains awake before God. In His presence truths are passed into the depths of the soul as the conscious mind sleeps. During sleep the defenses of the ego lie suspended. God communicates purely, soul to soul, as the dream happens. In the words of John Sanford, dreams are "God's forgotten language." Nothing stands between His divine revelation and the hungry heart. Denials, intellectualizations, resistances of all kinds fall away during the unbidden communications from the Lord of the kingdom within.

Interior matters relating to one's interpersonal relationships and to one's relationship with God surface through the medium of dream symbols. That is to say, each person, event, place, and scenario symbolize the interior state of the dreamer. Dark feelings such as rage, jealousy, greed, and pride are unearthed. His light shines into the dark recesses of the heart. The dream unveils the true emotional and spiritual climate of the soul.

A young woman once frantically ran up to me after a weekend seminar and demanded my immediate attention. She looked terrified

as she asked, "Is it possible that a dream could reveal that I am dying
from a disease? I mean, my dream last night said that I was filled up
with cancer. I was literally dying from cancer. I am horrified to think
that I could be so near death."

I quickly and firmly reminded her to avoid literalism in interpreting
dreams. In dreams, cancer refers to an affliction of soul. As we pur-
sued the matter, it became clear that unrelenting bitterness and rage
had been eating away at her for a number of years. Just as cancer eats
away at the body, so unresolved resentment eats away at the soul. The
dream plainly stated the truth: the cancer of rage had nearly killed
her. She needed immediate help. Fortunately, she entered into in-
depth psychotherapy with a Christian psychologist in her area, and
not a moment too soon.

Throughout scriptural history we witness God's revelation through
the dream. Fleeing from his homeland, Jacob felt the presence of God
and through a dream:

> And he dreamed that there was a ladder set up on the earth, and at the
> top of it reached to heaven; and behold, the angels of God were ascend-
> ing and descending on it! And behold, the Lord stood above it and said,
> "I am the Lord, the God of Abraham your father and the God of Isaac;
> the land on which you lie I will give to you and to your descendants;
> and your descendants shall be like the dust of the earth, and you shall
> spread abroad to the west and to the east and to the north and to the
> south; and by you and your descendants shall all the families of the
> earth bless themselves. Behold, I am with you and will keep you wher-
> ever you go, and will bring you back to this land; for I will not leave you
> until I have done that of which I have spoken to you." Then Jacob
> awoke from his sleep and said, "Surely the Lord is in this place; and I
> did not know it." (Gen. 28:12–16)

The dream reveals God's presence, a presence that may be covered
over to consciousness. Jacob needed the awareness of God's provision,
guidance, and presence. The dream ministered to him with the great
light of God's presence in the everlasting now.

St. Peter similarly encountered the presence of the living Jesus in
and through a dream:

> About noon, the following day as they were approaching the city, Peter
> went up on the roof to pray. He became hungry and wanted something
> to eat, and while the meal was being prepared, he fell into a trance. He

saw heaven open and something like a large sheet being let down to earth by its four corners. It contained all kinds of four-footed animals, as well as reptiles of the earth and birds of the air. Then a voice told him, "Get up, Peter. Kill and eat." "Surely no, Lord!" Peter replied. "I have never eaten anything impure or unclean." The voice spoke to him a second time, "Do not call anything impure that God has made clean." This happened three times, and immediately the sheet was taken back to heaven. (Acts 10:9–16)

This dream changed the course of salvation history for Jews and Gentiles. Because of the influence of this dream, St. Peter carried the gospel message to the house of Cornelius, a Gentile. Rather than reserving the message of salvation just for the Jews, Peter had been instructed by the dream, symbolically, to proclaim the gospel message with more understanding of the height, the depth, the width, and the length of God's love for all people. The dream brought light to his darkness.

St. Paul's ministry solidly developed in part as a result of guidance received from a dream:

And they went through the region of Phrygia and Galatia, having been forbidden by the Holy Spirit to speak the word in Asia. And when they had come opposite Mysia, they attempted to go into Bithynia, but the Spirit of Jesus did not allow them; so, passing by Mysia, they went down to Troas. And a vision appeared to Paul in the night: a man of Macedonia was standing beseeching him and saying, "Come over to Macedonia and help us." And when he had seen the vision, immediately we sought to go on into Macedonia, concluding that God had called us to preach the gospel to them. (Acts 16:6–10)

For St. Paul, God spoke to him in and through the dream. Without a doubt, his dream shed new light on his ministerial activities. Through the dream, he followed Jesus day by day in a new way.

I have been personally guided in important decisions in and through my dreams. Prior to deciding on where I would train during my residency in clinical psychology, I felt a great deal of conflict. My graduate committee urged me to attend one residency program, whereas I was in favor of another. A dream settled the issue.

One morning, the day before I needed to make my decision, I dreamed that I was right in the middle of Lake Michigan looking out onto the skyline of the city of Chicago. I sensed God's presence and calling in this dream. My doubts and conflicts subsided. I knew the will of God for me in this situation. I chose to attend Northwestern University School of Medicine and complete my residency in clinical psychology. While in Chicago, I met my analytic mentor, a man who greatly influenced the course of my personal and professional development. God's will became unquestionably clear to me as I listened to His voice spoken in and through a dream.

Through this experience, I learned the importance of the words of Jesus to St. Paul, "My grace is sufficient for you, for my power is made perfect in weakness" (2 Cor. 12:9). My doubt and confusion had rendered me helpless. At the moment in which my own willfulness no longer dominated my sensibilities, God could come through in this way.

In a sense, I needed to be rendered helpless in order to be helped by Him. Frequently, dreams appear during moments of crisis. The ego surrenders its power and acquiesces to the grace of God. In this manner, His grace is made perfect in our weakness.

A fifty-two-year-old man was referred to me by his pastor for a seemingly untreatable physical problem. He seemed to spontaneously lose his hearing at very inappropriate times. Various medical doctors could find no physiological explanation for his recurrent deafness.

As we looked deeper into the matter, it became very clear that he lost his hearing only in the presence of his mother-in-law. Whenever she entered a room, he would lose all of his hearing. He felt completely stupefied by this realization. He did not know what to make of it.

The night before our second session, he recorded the following dream: "I was in my childhood home talking with my mother. All of a sudden, her fingers grew to be ten feet long. She tangled her fingers around my neck and began to choke me. I could not breathe. I struggled and struggled to free myself from my mother."

As we peered into the meaning of the dream, he admitted that his mother, who had died some ten years before, had a choke-hold on him during his early years. In fact, he painfully verbalized that even now when he remembered her, he sometimes felt smothered. He also felt caged in and choked by the presence of his mother-in-law.

When she walked into a room she dominated everyone and everything with her incessant talking. He learned to tune her out. Whenever she sauntered into a room, he spontaneously lost his hearing and thereby felt free of her.

He enacted with his mother-in-law the pain that he actually felt toward his mother. The gradual working through of these feelings of anger and hurt toward his mother freed him from his hearing problem. Dealing with his feelings more truthfully also enabled him to be more direct and honest with his mother-in-law. She also became more respectful as he grew more forthright.

St. Paul in his letter to the Ephesians wrote, "For once you were darkness, but now you are light in the Lord" (5:8). Dreams reveal inner darkness that prompts one to grow toward the light. Movement toward the light of Christ heals past pains and unresolved conflicts. The healing light of Jesus vanquishes all darkness.

St. Paul continues, " . . . walk as children of light (for the fruit of light is found in all that is good and right and true), and try to learn what is pleasing to the Lord" (5:8–10). Dreams assist us in cooperating with the ongoing process of living as children of the light. The voice of God that comes during sleep prunes away unconscious and therefore thwarting emotions so that the fruit of the light may abound.

Inner goodness as described by St. Paul consists in loving the unlovable in an almost numinous and supernatural manner. Righteousness brings one into an undivided allegiance to God and the path of holiness. Truth inspires one to face inner and outer realities, knowing that God is always at work in and through every situation. Goodness, righteousness, and truth are the great enablers of the soul, allowing the very presence and power of God to flow freely. This manifestation deeply pleases the Lord as witnessed by the believer's inner contentment and continued progress in the spiritual life.

St. Paul exhorts us to an ever-steady wakefulness: " 'Awake, O sleeper, and arise from the dead, and Christ shall give you light' " (Eph. 5:14). Understanding dreams creates spiritual wakefulness. Death occurs when one no longer understands one's self and one's relationship with God. In such a case, the person becomes part of the living dead—physically alive but spiritually asleep.

When I first began my training as a depth psychologist, I dreamed of these very words quoted by St. Paul. The night before my first analytic session, I saw the words written in my dream: "Awake, O sleeper, and arise from the dead, and Christ shall give you light." Over the course of my personal experience in analysis I felt myself coming from death to life. Even though I had formally committed myself to Jesus and had been baptized in the Holy Spirit, certain

parts of my soul were still dormant and dead. As I listened to my
deepest feelings and dreams, the light of Christ shone in my soul,
producing great fruit and life.

The dream, therefore, is a living reality through which the Holy
emerges. Dream symbols act as the vessels that contain the presence
of the Holy. Every man and woman thus innately carries the potential to experience sacredness. The transforming presence of Jesus
arises out of the depths of the soul and imbues spirit, mind, and body
with life.

Grasping the personal meaning of a dream symbol produces stronger spiritual faith. A revealed holiness touches the soul with divine
inspiration. Herein egocentric concerns and selfish motives give way
to the will of God. In and through dreams God woos the soul ever-
more to Himself.

Just as I shared with you the dream that initiated my own analysis,
so I will candidly confess the dream that ended my analysis, one of
the most significant dreams of my life. In many ways, I hesitantly
confide in you. A dream of this intensity and personal meaning I
regard as sacred and not to be casually mentioned. I do appreciate
your sensitivity and understanding in this matter.

The night before one of my final analytic sessions, I had the following dream:

> A white-robed monk appeared to me. His robes were of an unearthly
> brilliance, his head was covered with a monk's cowl and bowed toward
> his heart as though in prayer. Once I realized his presence, he slowly
> looked up at me and said, "All is well with your soul."

As he said this, I felt his light and radiance rise up from within
me. The holiness of God saturated my soul. In the words of my analyst, "Our work together is now over. Your soul is well. You must now
daily walk the path of holiness." The numinosity, light, and holiness
of the white-robed monk deeply moves me to this very day.

Prayer: Launching Your Heart Toward God

Isaiah the prophet proclaims, "Have you not known? Have you not
heard? The Lord is the everlasting God, the Creator of the ends of
the earth" (40:28). All feelings, attitudes, and dreams come together

in deep prayer. Life's secrets unfold within the heart as He is experienced personally. Each and every moment of life holds the potential of a deep encounter with Him—a moment of deep prayer.

Since He is the everlasting God, He is in all things. All of life draws us toward Him if we have eyes to see, ears to hear, and a heart to understand. His inspiration calls for life out of the most negative of external situations and the most painful of inner feelings.

He creates; out of the good and the bad He creates. In His eyes, all things surrender to Him their fruit. Anger, guilt, and fear, as they are deeply understood, birth the presence of love. No longer does one need to flee from inner darkness. What seems so terrifying to face will bring growth and healing as long as one proceeds with the truth. In this case, dealing with and resolving painful feelings become a moment of prayer in which the loving presence of Jesus is present. A relationship based on facing truth, no matter how painful, is a gathering in His name—a creative encounter with the Holy.

A middle-aged Methodist woman came into my office beset with anxiety and worry over her teenage daughter. She complained, "I feel like she is losing her soul. She won't go to church any more. She won't attend Sunday school. I can't control her."

The mother's voice was fraught with anger and control. It became quite clear that the most pressing concern was that of being able to control and dominate her daughter. Even though she rightly desired that her daughter attend church, her manner of forcefulness and coerciveness was enough to drive away the saintliest of believers.

Once I spoke with her daughter, the real problem became more apparent. In her daughter's words, "I know that I love God. I think that God even loves me. But I just can't go to church. My mother smothers me. I feel drowned by her kind of faith. She's shoving God down my throat."

The anger between this mother and daughter stifled the presence of God in their relationship. The daughter, for the sake of her own emotional and spiritual health, needed distance from her mother. After a few months of counseling, the daughter's anger toward her mother began to lose its grip. The teenage girl began to attend another Methodist church that attracted a younger membership. In fact, she regularly attended services for many weeks before her mother realized what had happened. In her own way, she wanted to grow close to God.

When her mother found out, she felt befuddled. "I don't know what I am going to do with that girl. She still isn't doing what I told her. I still want her at my church. But I guess what is important is that she's following God in her way."

I replied simply, "God seems to have things under control in a way that meets your daughter where she is at. Your daughter's faith is, in a way, tailored to her. I am sure that we can trust God to continue seeing your daughter through now."

In each of my consultation sessions with this teenage girl, I felt the distinct presence of God. Her honesty and painstaking truthfulness caused us to experience a great deal of progress. The light of Christ shone easily due to her candor and genuineness. At the end of each session, I felt that we had faced truth and therein touched the face of God. Our relationship was a relationship of deep truth and therefore of deep prayer.

Deep prayer is experiencing God in the now. God's immanence flows through the daily occurrences of life. An ornate church, a hidden-away monastery, or a highly structured liturgical service is unnecessary to dwell fully in God. These external structures or observances may aid in inspiring the soul toward Him but are in no way requirements. God dwells in the now.

Isaiah the prophet proclaims, "His understanding is unsearchable. He gives power to the faint, and to him who has no might he increases strength. Even youths shall faint and be weary, and young men shall fall exhausted; but they who wait for the Lord shall renew their strength, they shall mount up with wings like eagles, they shall run and not be weary, they shall walk and not faint" (40:28–31).

The depths of God's understanding embrace moments of weakness, weariness, failure, and faintheartedness. God understands your pain. He understands your need. As you open up your heart to Him He will meet you in the now.

Realizing that there is no human emotion that God does not understand strengthens the most timid and anemic soul. Even though no one else may truly understand, God's capacity to feel deeply and have compassion stretches from sea to sea. Indeed, His breadth and depth of understanding with regard to human nature can be fully and completely relied upon. His caring and empathy are boundless. He knows what we attempt to hide. Often, through crisis and pain, one's inner being gradually and painfully yields darkness and egocentricity to God. At that moment, even the most egocentered individual feels the conviction of truth and the surety of God's understanding.

St. Anselm of Canterbury beautifully wrote of the inconceivable depth of God's understanding in the now:

> For how great is that light from which shines every truth that gives light to the rational mind? How great is that truth in which is everything that is true, and outside which is only nothingness and the false? How boundless is the truth that sees at one glance whatsoever has been made and by whom, and through whom, and how it has been made from nothing? What purity, what certainty, what splendor where it is? Assuredly, more than a creature can concede.

Unlocking the secret of God in the now opens the soul to new dimensions of growth. Hiding away from the light stunts personal growth; a candid and open relationship with others and God feasts the soul on true spiritual meat. God then activates the faculties of the soul and growth occurs. Such inner faculties include the capacity to experience love, the heartfelt perception of interior calm, and a sense of clear-mindedness.

St. Augustine eloquently describes this growth:

> Therefore, in the very mind, in the inner man, there is a sort of growth, not only to the passing from milk to meat, but also to the taking of that meat more and more abundantly. A growth, however, not in dimensions of size but in luminous intelligence; because the meat itself is intellectual light. That you may grow, then, and the more you grow, may receive more and more, you must ask in hope, not of the teacher who makes the sound in ears, who from without planteth and watereth, but of Him who giveth the increase.

The God of Comfort—The God of Glory

God's presence in the now flows through the experience of comfort and glory in deep prayer. These two anointings ready the Christian for life's inner and outer battles. In fact, they prove to be quite indispensable in striving to follow Him closely. These anointings act as a salve in the shouldering of daily burdens.

In his second letter to the Corinthians, St. Paul declares, "Blessed be the God and Father of our Lord Jesus Christ, the Father of mercies

and God of all comfort, who comforts us in all our affliction, so that
we may be able to comfort those who are in any affliction, with the
comfort with which we ourselves are comforted by God" (1:3–4).
God is a God of comfort. During trials and troubles His nature exudes
comfort. Outer tempests and inner turmoil leave the soul ready for
the fresh grace of comfort.

God always creates fresh blessings for new problems. Yesterday's
blessings never adequately meet today's problems. Just as the Israelites
in the desert required new manna for each new day, so the believer
must seek God for fresh blessings—fresh comfort for each new trial.
As manna flowed freely with each new day, so the believer must seek
God for fresh blessings—fresh comfort for each new problem comes
into the heart in unexpected moments as God is earnestly sought.

St. John of the Cross poetically articulated the beauty of divine
comfort in the soul:

> Oh living flame of love
> That tenderly wounds my soul
> In its deepest center! Since
> Now you are not oppressive,
> Now consummate! If it be your will:
> Tear through the veil of this sweet encounter!
>
> Oh sweet coutery
> Oh delightful wound!
> Oh gentle hand! Oh delicate touch
> That tastes of eternal life
> And pays every debt!   In killing You change death to life.
>
> Oh lamps of fire!
> In whose splendors
> The deep caverns of feeling,
> Once obscure and blind,
> Now give forth, so rarely, so exquisitely, both warmth
> and light to their Beloved.
>
> How gently and lovingly
> You waken my heart
> Where in secret you dwell alone;
> And in your sweet breathing,
> Filled with good and glory,
> How tenderly you swell my heart with love.

The God of comfort is also the God of glory. Jesus prayed for believers, "The glory which thou hast given me I have given to them,
that they may be one even as we are one, I in them and thou in
me . . . " (John 17:22–23). The experience of God is the experience
of glory. Glory and God go hand in hand.

Each evening my wife Kathy and I end our family prayer with the
recitation of the Our Father. At the conclusion, my daughter Maria
never fails to ask, "Dad, what does glory mean?" Each evening I reply, "Maria, glory means Jesus all over." Her face beams with joy at
my answer; together we share in this great secret of life that glory is
Jesus all over.

I refer to the experience of "Jesus all over" as a secret because it is
only as we press our ear against the Father's mouth that we hear his
secret whisperings. In quietness and stillness, He utters profound
truths of the faith. In knowing Him deeply, simple and life-changing
truth emerges from the depth of the soul: glory is Jesus all over.

With the realization that Jesus is in all things and holds all things
together, life exudes richness and meaning. Life is Jesus and Jesus is
life. All things find their meaning in Him. The work of your hands
becomes holy in Him. Intellectual endeavors become grace-filled in
Him. Spiritual ministries become anointed with the numinous, the
holy, in Him.

God in the now is more than enough. He is more than enough to
meet the practical needs of your life. He is concerned over your concerns. He shoulders your burdens. He is with you in the now . . .
with you in comfort. Jesus is all over you, all around you, in you, and
with you in glory. Jesus in the now is more than enough.

6

Deep Prayer: The Call Within

Encountering Jesus in deep prayer issues forth from answering the call within. Jesus beckons the believer to search intensely for and discover His presence interiorly. The practice of abiding in a continual awareness of Him, day and night and night and day, disposes the soul for a creative encounter with God. Uttering the name "Jesus" during waking hours, continually and unceasingly, so that even sleep seems to be filled with the soul's whispering of His name, creates a spiritual climate of abiding deep prayer.

Deep prayer, the experience of God in the everlasting now, assuredly can be discovered in moments of quiet understanding in human relationships, in and through the holy revelations contained in dreams and during formal prayer, but perhaps one of the most practical and powerful spiritual disciplines that warm the heart with deep prayer is the constant invocation of the name "Jesus." Heaven calls the soul to be more and more yielded to the Lord of glory. St. Paul in his letter to the Hebrews wrote, "Therefore, holy brethren, who share in a heavenly call, consider Jesus, the apostle and high priest of our confession" (3:1). The continual uttering of the name of Jesus fixes thoughts and feelings on Jesus and thus brings heaven to the soul and the soul to heaven. Deep prayer permeates the life of one whose lips never cease to whisper, "Jesus."

A caution must be noted here. A state of ceaseless prayer is born out of a free desire to draw closer to God rather than out of a neurotic compulsion to engage in a religious observance. An anxious and uptight recitation of the name of Jesus produces disharmony and contributes to what is in all probability an ongoing neurosis.

Guilt-ridden individuals tend to be rigid and compulsive with regard to expressions of faith. They perceive God as a cold taskmaster who demands oblations and prayers. Their prayers are woven emo-

126

tionally and spiritually with self-condemnation. Such an individual might be tempted to use the Jesus Prayer in a self-destructive manner. When stress, personal turmoil, and compulsion characterize the use of the Jesus Prayer, it should be laid aside until a spiritual director or Christian psychologist can provide appropriate guidance. God is a God not of unrelenting demands but of compassion, freedom, and glory.

Transformation into Freedom

Danger seems greatest when divine freedom is closest. Freedom strikes many individuals as a much-desired and sought-after state of mind; however, true freedom actually can be quite frightening. Inner liber-ation means that blame for life-problems and challenges can no longer be levied upon those with whom one lives. Fault-finding, crit-icizing, moaning and groaning over the tribulations of everyday life serve no purpose once an individual finds freedom and assumes re-sponsibility for his or her life. True freedom dawns with both enthu-siasm and responsibility . . . perhaps a very frightening prospect.

"Now the Lord is the Spirit, and where the Spirit of the Lord is, there is freedom" (2 Cor. 3:17). Jesus is spirit and dwells within us as spirit. His presence can be felt within as a particular quality of release from oppression, negative and egocentric attitudes, and a downheart-edness toward self and others. He is the liberator par excellence who bequeaths help, healing, and freedom in greater and greater measure to those who abide in Him.

Spirit communicates to spirit all that is whole and holy, all that brings peace of mind and personal autonomy. Rather than coercing His followers to fall into line, He instead encourages self-expression, individualism, and personal creativity. These fruits of freedom then bind like-minded souls together into a tightly knit community of faith. The freedom of Jesus within draws people to Jesus and people to people.

Solid spiritual communities emerge from this deep heavenly en-counter. Freedom rather than force unites believer to believer with a bond that endures forever. Once legalism and rulings replace a free coming-together, community degenerates and institutionalism begins. Rigid rules and set ways of thinking thwart the free flow of the spirit of Jesus. Only His spirit freely experienced, freely shared, and freely lived creates real church—the gathering together of believers who are of one heart and one mind in the knowledge of Him who has set them free.

But as mentioned previously, freedom oftentimes entails a perception of great threat on the horizon. Unity with self and others brings a death to narcissism and onesided individualism. Not only does one have to forsake personal ambitions and other such ego-enhancing activities so that the welfare of all might be predominant, but in actuality one must be willing to feel the loss that may accompany freedom.

Old but familiar and well-worn lifestyles may no longer be in keeping with spiritual liberation. Only that which is loving and creative can partake of emotional liberty and victory. This is not to say that darker emotions such as anger and fear are left undealt with or perhaps even blatantly denied; rather, dark attitudes are approached directly and forthrightly, resulting in relief and constructive resolution. No human being can ever be rendered invulnerable to dark emotions. All things, however, serve in the end to create new life and thus foster the resurrection power of the living Christ within the heart.

"The spirit of the Lord God is upon me, because the Lord has anointed me to bring good tidings to the afflicted; he has sent me to bind up the brokenhearted, to proclaim liberty to the captives, and the opening of the prison to those who are bound" (Isa. 61:1). Freedom from captivity is at the heart of the good news proclaimed by Jesus. Without such an experience, one can never be said to have fully encountered the risen Christ.

Some individuals have attended church, received the sacraments, listened faithfully to homilies, all without ever having felt released from their captivity. External observances such as these at most only make one available to the spirit of freedom. Religious rituals do not in and of themselves guarantee that the bondage of personal oppression will be broken.

Jesus referred to the fact that the Father had "anointed" Him, the original Greek word used in the New Testament being *chriō*. This word uniformly refers to an anointing with the Holy Spirit in the heart of the believer. In the Old Testament, priests and kings were inducted into office by a process of anointing with oil. Now, all believers have been anointed with the Holy Spirit and carry His presence within and are thus holy and completely anointed into the priesthood of Jesus. The Holy Spirit takes up permanent residence within the heart and provides all that is necessary spiritually and emotionally to live and serve in an uninhibited Christlike manner. The anointing of the Spirit dwells in the Christian experientially and leads to deeper encounters with Jesus, who is freedom.

Encountering God through His anointing within begins the process of transformation into freedom. A living relationship with the risen Jesus disentangles unhealthy relationships, works through negative attitudes and bad habits, and inspires greater fidelity to the inner walk with Him. It is then that religious observances can be filled with solace and nourishment.

Once the foundation of the anointing by the Holy Spirit has been established experientially, external observances can now nurture inner growth. With such a living relationship with God leaders in the Christian community inspire, not force, the coming together of believers. The deep well of the Holy Spirit is an anointing within the heart that plentifully satisfies the ever-present thirst of the believer for more of Him. At one and the same time, the disciple of Jesus feels satisfied and yet thirsts and hungers for more, more of Him who is all in all, more of Him who has freely called and freely loved. Transformation into such an intense and well-grounded freedom characterizes both the individual believer and the inspired coming-together of the faithful.

Tom, a forty-seven-year-old churchgoing man, practiced the invocation of the name of Jesus twice per day, twenty minutes in the morning and twenty minutes in the evening, in quietness and solitude. He also maintained a near-constant perception of God's presence via the utterance of the name of Jesus quietly throughout the day. His work as a researcher in biochemistry gave him ample opportunity to invoke quietly, in whispering tones, the name of Jesus throughout the day. Moments of great consolation and tranquillity filled his heart.

One morning, after meditating on the name of Jesus, a sudden anxiety overtook him. For no apparent reason, a sense of dread and tension took hold of his innermost being. Throughout the day, he felt periodic waves of worry and fear. Even after his evening meditation, the tension persisted. Completely befuddled, he prayed again before retiring, hoping somehow to find release in sleep.

That night, he dreamed that a demon was threatening to destroy him. He saw himself in a cold, dark room about to be pounced upon by a dark and seemingly demonic force. In the dream, he shook and trembled with fear. The more he uttered the name of Jesus, the closer the demon seemed to come.

I saw Tom the following day at a retreat that I was conducting. He felt positive that he needed an immediate exorcism. A demon of some sort, he felt, must be oppressing him from within. Once he settled down I asked him to consider another alternative.

We talked over the fact that dreams speak a symbolic language. Frequently, the experience of deep prayer, such as is found in uttering the name of Jesus throughout the day, surfaces hidden feelings and unresolved conflicts. We need not be afraid of this sort of uncovering. It is the hand of God at work cleansing the soul.

As we both explored the personal meaning of this supposed demon, he suddenly exclaimed, "The demon reminds me of death. Plain death. I felt like if it got a hold of me it would kill me. The more I said the name of Jesus, the closer it got."

We finally realized that by not taking death literally, we could understand its deeper significance. In this case, death referred to dying to old and selfish attitudes and behaviors. Death did not refer to a literal and physical death. God was calling him to forsake a very self-destructive inner attitude.

As we discussed this, he became aware of his fright, indeed his panic, over the prospect of change. God's voice, in and through the dream, called him to grow up and let go of his tendency toward emotional withdrawal and hesitant self-expression. These new feelings frightened him and he resisted their flow. He had become comfortable with his emotional withdrawal and aloofness. God now required more—more love and more warmth.

Tom remarked, "You see, I'd never really extended myself to other people. I stayed locked up inside myself. In many ways, it's the only thing I've ever known. Now, it is time to grow up and die to this old self-centered attitude. As I have deepened my walk with God, I am not as afraid of other people as I used to be. The closer I feel to God, the more comfortable I am with others. The demon in my dreams was really a symbol of the death that needed to take place within me. It is truly the spirit of God at work."

In the months to come, Tom continued his practice of the Jesus Prayer during quiet times and throughout the day. He gradually found himself, quite spontaneously, communicating more with others. Those closest to him remarked that he seemed to come alive. No longer did he come across as a cold fish; now he grew to relate to others in a more and more personable and compassionate manner.

Deep prayer, the unceasing utterance of the name of Jesus, surfaced new and creative personal growth. Tom felt transformed and set free as he practiced the presence of God throughout the day. Freedom means growth and growth means freedom. Jesus embodies the fullness of freedom and gives freely to those who diligently seek Him.

I recall the diligence of blind Bartimaeus. Jesus and His disciples had ministered in the city of Jericho throughout the day. Large crowds gathered around Him and His disciples as He was leaving the city. Nearby sat the blind beggar, Bartimaeus.

"And when he heard that it was Jesus of Nazareth, he began to cry out, 'Jesus, son of David, have mercy on me!' " (Mark 10:47). Even though Bartimaeus could not see Jesus with his physical eyes, he beheld him with the eyes of his soul. He felt the presence of Jesus of Nazareth. Jesus lives within and those who see Him most clearly see Him within and constantly utter "Lord . . . Jesus."

The large crowd of people standing over Bartimaeus rebuked him for shouting out to Jesus. They ordered him to be quiet. In their minds, a blind beggar had no business calling out to Jesus of Nazareth. The more they attempted to suppress him the more loudly Bartimaeus shouted, "Son of David, have mercy on me!"

Despite all outer obstacles and criticisms by others, God is on your side. He wants to come through for you, if you will but press forward, not allowing anything or anyone to stand between you and Him. He wants you to experience Him in the now as you call upon his name without ceasing. Great persistence and diligence paved the way for greater depths of healing.

Finally, Jesus stopped and said, "Call him." All of the people yelled out to Bartimaeus, "Cheer up! On your feet! He's calling you." Without hesitation, Bartimaeus jumped up and walked to Jesus.

One must remember that Bartimaeus, a blind man, found his own way to Jesus. Hundreds of people surrounded him, stood between him and Jesus. The scriptures do not indicate that anybody helped him to find Jesus. As he gazed upon the presence of Jesus within, he encountered Him in the external world.

Jesus knew that great faith requires unyielding determination. Jesus required that Bartimaeus find his way. Jesus did not rush over to Bartimaeus and attempt to pamper him. He expected Bartimaeus to do his part, to give his all, so that God could then give His all.

" 'What do you want me to do for you?' Jesus asked him. And the blind man said to him, 'Master, let me receive my sight.' And Jesus said to him, 'Go your way; your faith has made you well.' And immediately he received his sight and followed him on the way" (Mark 10:51–52).

Unceasingly calling upon the name of Jesus heals spiritual blindness, opening the eyes of the soul to the love of God. True freedom exists in discovering the love of God as a free gift. Divine love experienced within the soul requires only constant reaching out: "Jesus, Son of David, have mercy on me . . . Jesus . . . Lord Jesus."

Transformation into Glory

Kathy and I quietly slipped into a Mexican restaurant in downtown Albuquerque after having spent the afternoon teaching and ministering in a healing service. During our presentation we emphasized that as God heals the soul, manifestations of actual physical healing may also take place. This three-hour service left us filled up with God, relaxed in body and soul, and ready for dinner.

In the restaurant's waiting area sat a family of five or six. One of the women in the group looked at us as though caught by surprise when we entered the restaurant. After some hesitation she approached us. It seemed as though she sincerely wanted to tell us something.

"Dr. DeBlassie, you and your wife helped me to find God in a new way today. I feel that the very glory of God has touched my soul and my body. For six months I have been in constant pain. The best orthopedic surgeons had been unable to alleviate this horrible discomfort. My back felt like someone was hammering on it and, at the same time, poking it with little pins. The pain was excruciating.

"I don't know exactly when it happened, but at some point one of your prayer ministers came up to me, placed her hand on my back and prayed with me. I felt completely filled and surrounded by God. I know His glory. I've touched it. I was literally caught up into God.

"About fifteen minutes later I realized that I was pain-free. It caught me by surprise. The glory of God so occupied my mind that I forgot about my pain—so much so that I hadn't even realized that I had been healed. I feel closer to God now. This is the first time I have felt relief at all in over six months. God touched me with His glory today."

God's glory, experienced during a moment of deep prayer, causes inner and outer transformation. The Gospel of Matthew records that Jesus healed those suffering from severe pain (4:24). Jesus heals the body as the soul is caught up into His glory. Deep prayer of this sort seems to take one by surprise. Conscious worries and concerns fade away when one is consumed with Christ Jesus—the hope of glory.

An intense experience of God's presence can occur in a group setting in which those present ardently seek God. Herein faith enkindles faith and the presence of God becomes manifest in a powerful manner. Whether this is a genuine experience of deep prayer or is merely an emotional high depends upon the fruit such an experience bears.

The first epistle of John states, "Beloved, do not believe every spirit, but test the spirits to see whether they are of God" (4:1). An experience of emotional inflation can easily be confused with a genuine encounter with God. An inauthentic experience reeks of emotional flightiness, a will-to-power, and an insensitivity toward others. Groups of people coming together to induce spiritual experience run the risk of bearing this sort of bad fruit. Dissensions, rivalries, gossip, and backbiting result from the puffed-up feelings accompanying an experience of spirits other than the Holy Spirit.

True deep prayer produces greater truth within. Egocenteredness and personal insensitivity give way to humility and self-knowledge. Unconditional love and understanding bespeak a deep encounter with the living God.

The woman healed of back pain came to me many months later attesting to her new-found and stable spiritual devotion. She shared, "Throughout the day I feel drawn to utter the name 'Jesus.' I live in Him all day long. Every time I say His name, my heart glows with spiritual fervor. I desire only Him."

She also recounted transformations occurring in her family relationships. As a result of her inner experience and consequent physical healing, conflicted family relationships began to be healed. She sensed a new ability to understand the hurts and pains of her children. Formerly she had frequently dismissed their feelings with a curt response. "Oh, you'll get over it." Such lack of understanding bruised her children. They gradually withdrew from her and did their own thing. Eventually this degenerated into rebelliousness, drug abuse, and chronic fighting.

Her intense faith experience during the healing conference produced a new fervor for the love of God and the love of others. She cooperated with this grace by maintaining a life of deep prayer. Throughout the day she uttered the name "Jesus." Thus, the authenticity of this spiritual encounter can be attested to by the fruit borne in her life: physical pain subsided never to return, family relationships improved very gradually but surely, and personal spiritual devotion and discipline continued for the months and years to come.

The Breath of Jesus

When Jesus breathes his breath into the soul, one feels both transformed and inspired. Moments of divine infilling stir within and create newness without. From inspirations come ideas, ministries, projects that contribute to the betterment of humankind, and the desire to grow deeper in Jesus through disciplined spiritual practice. The call within is a call to fresh inspiration—a new feeling of being alive in God.

Sally, a middle-aged typist, responded to the call within by whispering the name of Jesus unnoticeably throughout her workday and evening. As a very proficient typist, she produced quality work in such a smooth and efficient manner that she could completely attend to and concentrate on the task at hand while still focusing on the name of Jesus. As she would breathe in, she would quietly whisper, "Lord." Upon exhalation, she imperceptibly pronounced, "Jesus." From eight to five and on into the night, she called upon His name.

Even though she maintained this ardent and disciplined devotion, she felt beset by a tormenting problem. The thought of being alone terrified her. She irrationally anticipated that being alone during a time of prayer would meet with horrible consequences. Somehow, in some way, she expected that God would not be present. She could pray all day long, as long as someone else was in the room, and this included even the presence of a dog or a cat—just as long as some living presence was with her. Left all alone with God, she feared that He would not be present with her. She would show up, but God would not or so she feared.

Finally, after six months of practicing the Jesus Prayer throughout the day, she felt compelled to go into her bedroom, alone, and utter His name. Great love for Him prompted her finally to take the

chance of being alone with the Great Alone. That evening after
work, she went into her bedroom, practically shaking and trembling.
Alone in her room she sat quietly and pronounced the name "Jesus."

A sudden tranquillity overtook her. The peace of God entered into
her soul and body so profoundly that she drifted into a very light and
momentary sleep. Although she was not conscious of her surroundings, she was aware of continuing to utter the name of Jesus.

Suddenly, in a dreamlike fashion, she found herself on a beach.
With the sun shining and the waves rolling in, she breathed deeply.
As she breathed in, she breathed in the name and presence of Jesus.
As she breathed out, she exhaled fear and anxiety. Over and over
she, in this deep state of prayer, breathed in His presence and exhaled
fear and anxiety. Over and over again she released her inner torment
and drew in the presence of Jesus, the Lord of peace.

Some twenty minutes later, she came to her senses and realized
that she had been in this restful state uttering the name of Jesus for
quite a long period of time. Not only that, but she had been alone—
alone with the Great Alone. God showed up. God met her when she
came to meet Him in quiet and aloneness.

Sally remarked to me seven or eight days later that she no longer
feared aloneness. Jesus inspired her with Himself. As she yielded to
Him, and only to Him, in and through aloneness with Him, healing
filled her. The name of Jesus, constantly on her lips, blessed Sally
with the inspiration that literally healed and changed her life.

Inspiration into Crucifixion

Sally's inspiration into crucifixion necessitated death to her egocentric concerns. Jesus desires to be Lord over all facets of life, including
fear-ridden thoughts and attitudes. Not admitting and understanding
deeply held anxieties freezes the power of the crucifixion to take hold
within the soul. Jesus Christ, and Him crucified, unleashes incredible
healing energy as darkness within is faced and crucified.

Within Christian circles I have felt grave concern with regard to
the understanding of crucifixion. No one naturally desires to experience crucifixion. The willingness to undergo crucifixion comes as a
result of pure inspiration. God's grace enables human nature to embrace crucifixion, an activity of the soul that normally would be con-

sidered repulsive. God grants heavenly grace to those willing to die to
old and destructive egocentricities.

The death process of crucifixion does not occur through denying
negative emotions and interior states. Denial serves only to keep spiritual and emotional toxins hidden away. The poisons of mind and
spirit then continue to spread. Closing one's eyes to dark realities
does not do away with them; instead they insidiously crawl through
the soul unchecked.

Encountering interior darkness is not a one-time affair. Even with
extraordinary grace, deeply held unresolved emotions often take
many months or years to be fully integrated and healed. Concen-
trated grace, experienced during moments of deep prayer, accelerates
the ongoing process of inner healing. What may have transpired over
a lifetime, or perhaps may never have been transformed and healed in
this life, occurs gradually but surely over months and years with the
willingness to undergo crucifixion. The facing of truth, day by day,
prompts both crucifixion and the healing power of the resurrection to
be experienced within on a daily basis. Thus, quite ironically for us as
Christians, crucifixion and resurrection occur in close proximity and
yet span a lifetime—indeed, an eternity.

The story is told of the Desert Father Abba John. The holy father
prayed that all inner conflict and struggle with darkness would be
removed. He desired to feel free from care. He anticipated that he
could reach the state in which all interior crucifixion would be complete. Finally, he felt that he had achieved this state of no struggle,
no cares, no conflict. He confided about this to a holy man many
years his senior.

Abba John shared, "At last, I find myself completely at peace,
without struggle or concern, with no enemy." The older holy man
said to him, "Go quickly and ask God to stir up warfare within you.
Without struggle and constant crucifixion, you will lose your humility and constant dependence upon Him. It is by warfare that the soul
makes progress."

Abba John speedily returned to his prayer hut and beseeched God
to allow the necessary warfare to take place within him. He no longer
cried out for relief from struggles and conflict, for in these God's
grace grew within his soul. He now prayed only, "Lord, give me
strength for the fight."

God has placed within the soul the ability to struggle and overcome any and all trials. This is the true nature of crucifixion that

leads to wholeness and completeness. Psychological and spiritual wholeness does not manifest itself in some sort of static peacefulness. Activity, in harmony with the activity of God, generates holiness and wholeness. Inert passivity, a seeming freedom from struggle and inner crucifixion, stagnates and deadens the human heart. Life, continually renewed and replenished, involves conflict and struggle. God abundantly blesses not with a decaying conflict-free passivity, but with an unending anointing to undergo crucifixion with an ever-active hope calling us forward into Him.

In the words of the prophet Isaiah, "You whom I took from the ends of the earth, and called from its farthest corners, saying to you, 'You are my servant, I have chosen you and not cast you off; fear not, for I am with you, be not dismayed, for I am your God; I will strengthen you, I will help you, I will uphold you with my victorious right hand' " (41:9–10).

Inspiration into Faith

Not only does crucifixion depend upon divine inspiration, but faith as well requires God's presence to be actualized and felt. That is to say, only through the inspiration of Jesus does the latent gift of faith, residing in each Christian, become actualized. A new breath of God frees creative powers to imagine the unimaginable and achieve the unachievable. As a gift, faith is bequeathed into the soul.

The constant repetition of the name "Jesus" readies the soul for divine faith-filling. Unceasing prayer deeply immerses one into the presence of God so that the soul partakes of His nature which is intrinsically faith-filled. The very personality of God exudes positive and life-giving faith. The utterance of the name "Jesus" creates a communion with the very Heart of all faith. The divine Heart transmits faith to the human heart each time the name of Jesus is pronounced.

St. Paul wonderfully proclaimed, " . . . faith working though love" (Gal. 5:6). Frequently, one's focus on the essentials of life fades away amid the distractions of everyday living. St. Paul's intense living of the Christian life demarcated the only thing that truly counts.

Nothing else save faith expressing itself through love matters. In our context faith refers to the wholehearted yielding to each moment of deep prayer. Surrendering one's self completely to Him, in and through deep prayer, is an act of faith. In the end, nothing else counts save a life fully lived in and through a loving faith.

A conscious faith in God expresses itself in and through love. Instead of cold-hearted dogmatic proclamations, opinionated doctrines, and legalism, real faith becomes manifest in and through human caring and compassion. Herein the individual soul feels understood and unconditionally accepted. Not all actions, lifestyles, and attitudes may be condoned; but the sacredness of personal integrity and the struggle always to understand the human heart more deeply is the gift of the faith-filled.

St. Catherine of Siena recorded her inspirations on this matter:

> "I require that you should love Me with the same love with which I love you. This, indeed, you cannot do, because I love you without being loved. All the love which you have from Me you owe to Me, so that it is not of grace that you love Me, but because you ought to do so, while I love you out of grace and not because I owe you My love. Therefore, to me, in person, you cannot repay the love which I require of you, and I have placed you in the midst of your fellows, that you may do to them that which you cannot do to Me, that is to say, that you may love your neighbor of free grace, without expecting any return from him, and what you do to him I count as done to Me . . . "

Inspiration into Resurrection

The call within inspires one toward crucifixion, faith, and ultimately toward resurrection. Crucifixion and faith ready the soul to receive the fullness of the resurrection power won by Christ Jesus through His own death and resurrection. Faithfully enduring pain, trials, and suffering cleanses one interiorly and enables the grace of God to release new life. Resurrection power is an interior spring of healing water that helps to create and sustain emotional and spiritual health.

Sister Beatrice, a Roman Catholic nun of thirty years, quietly came to know resurrection inspiration in her own life. She recalled, "For nearly a decade, I was involved in the great charismatic denial. I call it the great charismatic denial because when I profoundly felt the presence of God in the Catholic charismatic movement, I quickly gave in to the belief that nothing should ever or could ever trouble my soul. Knowing Jesus meant that everything was taken care of—no more pain and no more struggle. When I did feel distressed and out of sorts, I never mentioned it. Others in my charismatic group might consider me less than spiritual. I denied the workings of the cross in my life."

Sister Beatrice presented herself as mild-mannered but forthright woman. She had participated very actively in the Catholic charismatic renewal for approximately ten years. During this time, she had participated in various pastoral responsibilities. On the surface, all looked well.

What no one realized was that beneath her charismatic talk and extroverted prayer lay a very hurting soul. A darkness that no one imagined grew within her. Throughout her life she suffered from a severe lack of affection that led to excessive fantasizing about sexual encounters. This eventually led to a sexual liaison with a priest in a neighboring state.

Never did she even consider confiding in someone about this dilemma. Denial, not painstaking truthfulness, was promulgated in her prayer group. Members of her charismatic prayer meeting emphasized focusing on Jesus in lieu of honesty in relationships. This thought maintained that a total investment in God demanded an almost total otherworldliness and rejection of human feelings. They considered emotions to be intrusive rather than nurturous of spiritual growth. Sister Beatrice gradually but definitely bought into this lie.

Inspiration toward resurrection never precedes inspiration to crucifixion and faith. The truth must be confronted, in an often painful manner, before interior freedom takes hold. Faith aids the individual in wading through the times of often horrendous crucifixion. Seeing inner truth crucifies the inner lies that propagate human misery. Resurrection then ensues.

The superior of her religious order finally found out about Sister Beatrice's illicit relationship. After three hours of intense conversation, they agreed that this hidden affair had been prompted by long-held unrecognized needs for affection and love. Sister Beatrice's pain overwhelmed her. With the support of her religious order, she entered into a year-long intensive program of treatment for distressed clergy and religious.

She told me, "Actually, I felt relieved that I had been found out. I invested an enormous amount of energy in hiding from the truth. My spirituality had even enabled me to cover up this inner battle.

My worship was so external that it never touched my soul. Finally, I was ready to take the journey within."

After her extensive program and intensive follow-up psychotherapy, resurrection power coursed through her soul. Rather than denying emotional vulnerabilities, she now candidly expressed her deepest feelings. She remarked to a group of novices, "God truly inspired me to do the soul work that I have done in these past two years. My daily prayer life sustained me and filled me with fresh inspiration to see the journey through. I somehow feel that now I will not lessen in my desire to grow and experience change."

One of the novices asked Sister Beatrice and a number of other nuns present what they did when feelings of distress or other problems weighed them down. One sister remarked, "I take a long walk—I walk and walk until I feel better." Another elderly nun replied. "I just get busy around the convent and start cleaning. Once everything looks clean, I feel better too." The superior of the order asserted, "All you have to do when you feel bad is take your rosary and go before Jesus in the tabernacle. Stay before Jesus in the tabernacle praying your rosary until your feelings go away. This always helps me and it will help you too."

Finally, Sister Beatrice shared, "I believe in Jesus in the tabernacle but, even more importantly, I believe in Jesus in the now. When I feel bad, I find a friend whom I trust and know will keep my confidence. We talk and share together. Once I feel understood, after having shared my feelings, I sense the presence of God—Jesus in the now."

St. Peter writes of this resurrection power, "Blessed be the God and Father of our Lord Jesus Christ! By his great mercy we have been born anew to a living hope through the resurrection of Jesus Christ from the dead, and to an inheritance which is imperishable, undefiled, and unfading, kept in heaven for you, who by God's power are guarded through faith for a salvation ready to be revealed in the last time" (1 Pet. 1:3–5).

The resurrection of Jesus inspires a new birth, a birth that inflames the soul with an alive hope. Such a never-ending hope sees one through the storms, the inevitable tribulations of day-to-day life. As faithfulness is maintained through crucifixion, resurrection is sure to follow. All that is required is the willingness to endure crucifixion and maintain faith in Jesus in the now.

The ever-present reality of God is beautifully expressed in the story of "The Talkative Lover":

A lover pressed his suit unsuccessfully for many months, suffering the atrocious pains of rejection. Finally, his sweetheart yielded. "Come to such and such a place, at such and such an hour," she said to him.

At that time and place, the lover finally found himself seated beside his beloved. He then reached into his pocket and pulled out a sheaf of love letters that he had written to her over the past months. They were passionate letters, expressing the pain he felt and his burning desire to experience the delights of love in union. He began to read them to his beloved. The hours passed by but still he read on and on.

Finally the woman said, "What kind of fool are you? These letters are all about me and your longing for me. Well, here I am sitting with you at last and you are lost in your stupid letters."

Anthony DiMello comments on this story, "Here I am with you," says God, "and you keep reflecting about me in your head, talking about me with your tongue, and searching for me in your books. When will your shut up and see?"

Perhaps this was the plight of the apostles in witnessing the resurrection of Jesus: "Now on the first day of the week, Mary Magdalene came to the tomb early, while it was still dark, and saw that the stone had been taken away from the tomb. So she ran, and went to Simon Peter and the other disciple, the one whom Jesus loved, and said to them, 'They have taken the Lord out of the tomb, and we do not know where they have laid him!" (John 20:2).

Resurrection power rolls the stone away from the tomb. That is to say, the tomb of negative and dead attitudes, miserable feelings, and egocentric desires is abandoned. Divine inspiration propels the soul out of this corrupt and inert state. With the breath of God breathed into the soul, interior hardness rolls away. Such a spiritual discovery creates great excitement: "Peter then came out with the other disciple, and they went toward the tomb. They both ran, but the other disciple outran Peter and reached the tomb first; and stooping to look in, he saw the linen cloths lying there, but he did not go in. Then Simon Peter came, following him, and went into the tomb; he saw the linen cloths lying, and the napkin, which had been on his head, not lying with the linen cloths but rolled up in a place by itself" (John 20:3–7).

Upon first encountering the numinous, one reacts with either an impulsive sort of yielding or a caught-off-guard fright. At one and the same time, we feel the inner urge to give ourselves over fully to Jesus in the now; yet a spontaneous reserve may dampen our desires, for the Holy is not under our control. The Holy draws us to it, to Him who is the source of all resurrection. We do not come to Him out of our own power. We come to Him because we are drawn to come by His grace and only by His grace. The thought of our lack of control in all of this can indeed cause a sudden gasp. As with John, we often require a few moments to get hold of ourselves, to realize that we are standing on holy ground, and take the next step—a step into resurrection.

"Then the other disciple, who reached the tomb first, also went in, and he saw and believed" (John 20:8).

Deliverance from Evil: Isolationism vs. Relationship

The call within, to deep prayer, leads ultimately to intense union with the Trinity and to simultaneous deliverance from evil. As the presence of God is ushered into the soul, the presence of evil departs. God requires light, yieldedness, and consciousness. To all of these, evil is opposed. Evil flees from the holiness encountered in deep prayer.

In answering the call within, the Christian comes face to face with evil. Jesus encountered the reality of evil after having been drawn into the fullness of the Spirit. "And Jesus, full of the Holy Spirit, returned from the Jordan, and was led by the Spirit for forty days in the wilderness, tempted by the devil" (Luke 4:1–2).

Evil is more than the absence of good. The doctrine of *privatio boni* only partially expresses the nature of the powerful reality known as evil. In point of fact, evil is more than the absence of the good. Evil exists as an independent reality opposed to all that is light, all that is conscious, all that is truth. Indeed, the evil one is the father of darkness, the father of unconsciousness, the father of lies.

Satan tempted Jesus: " 'If you are the Son of God, command this stone to become bread.' Jesus answered, 'It is written, "Man shall not live by bread alone" ' " (Luke 4:3–4).

Satan attempts to capture the soul via isolationism. Psychologically, changing the stone into bread symbolizes a train of thought that can possess one and propagate the lie that isolating oneself is the surest path to God. A stone stands alone. The "me and Jesus" type of spirituality leaves one convinced that people stand in the way of true spiritual growth. This deceitful perception demands an emotional coldness and personal aloofness, a stoniness of heart in which the individual believes that his or her isolated soul is spiritually strong and well nurtured. Beware . . . for in such a stone there is no bread.

In a sense, this temptation pushes for an identification with the Holy. The devil demanded that Jesus exhibit His spiritual power. Satan wanted Jesus to identify with the Father and use this spiritual power for selfish ends. In such isolationism, Jesus would have felt Himself to be above humankind, just Him and the Father, in need of no one or nothing else. This sort of isolationism creates extreme vulnerability to possession by evil.

Hiding oneself away from others of necessity causes evil to flourish. One caught in an isolated rut blows emotional injuries out of proportion. Without the feedback of interpersonal conversation, personal hurts and pains run round and round in the mind. Dwelling negatively on personal injuries saturates the soul with bleakness, since there seems to be no way out.

One so isolated gradually sinks into a well of despair. Hope results from the feeling that others care and can be relied upon. Without the sense of being emotionally connected to people, nihilism rots the roots of the soul. Caving in under the weight of nihilism throws the individual into the dungeons of evil. The god of all hopelessness trods upon such a soul with feelings of unrelenting misery and anguish. Truly, hell is the place of despair upon despair . . . neverending despair.

Jesus plainly knew the critical importance of fellowship. Two or three gathered in His name dilute evil's power. Conversation and dialogue eventually surface the truth. Listening one to another, people have the potential to sort through the most horrible of intrapsychic pains. When this happens, the individual no longer feels alone and therefore feels hope.

Hope unquestionably flows with deep prayer. Experiencing the presence of God, especially with others, powerfully generates a positive anticipation of God's providence. The simple utterance of the name of Jesus in faith exudes with life-giving expectation of good things to come. This obliterates evil's stronghold, since nihilism and

hope are mutually exclusive. The presence of Christ Jesus, the hope
of glory, quickly banishes the antics of the evil one.

Tom, a forty-five-year-old disabled electrician, lived in an isolated
apartment hidden away from family and friends. After an on-the-job
accident that inflicted permanent damage to his lower back, he acquired the means to live without working. On the subsidy of monthly
disability payments, he enclosed himself in a world of sterility and
isolation.

Since he had never married, he had no concern with regard to a
wife or children. The majority of his extended family lived in another
state. He cultivated no relationships at work. His weekly attendance
at Mass was a superficial gesture of religious observance. He would
come in late, sit at the back of the church, and leave right after
Communion each and every Sunday. This assured him that he would
be left alone without the interruption of speaking to another person.

In a rather convoluted way, Tom thought that hiding away from
people would protect him from pain. In his mind, this would enable
him freely and in an undistracted way to draw closer to God. He did,
in fact, spend a number of hours each day in prayer and writing in his
spiritual journal.

As the months passed by, Tom recalled that a gradual malaise began to afflict him. Rather that drawing nearer to God, he felt great
spiritual aridity and desolation. As time wore on, he grew more and
more depressed. A sickness of soul possessed him.

Tom confided, "I thought that if I made myself hard like a rock, I
would never have to feel hurt or rejected by other people. I lived
away from people. I saw no one and talked with no one. For over a
year I lived this way. And now, I feel hopeless. When I left people, I
left God."

Through severe detachment from people, Tom yielded to the temptation to isolate himself, to harden his heart, ostensibly to find real
happiness and love. At first he indeed felt no pain. No one was
around to pain him. After a while, he realized that not only did he
feel no pain, but in fact that he also felt nothing at all. The great
isolation of being a rock, an island, with no feelings and no pain,
afforded a brief respite from everyday struggles but in the end tormented him with despair.

After two years of intensive psychotherapy, Tom's life had notice-
ably improved. Our patient inner work helped him to work through
deeply held fears and terrors of the soul. Gradually, he warmed up to

people. The despair that had engulfed his soul no longer laid hold of him. Evil, real evil, lost its grip on Tom.

Withdrawal from human relationships left Tom without the healing balm of human understanding. I believe that evil capitalized on this. Since Satan authors all despair, I believe Satan oppressed Tom. Under the guise of an ascetic spirituality of avoidance, Satan duped Tom. Only by turning to another human being, someone who would care and understand, was Tom freed and delivered from evil. This occurred during the intensity of our psychotherapeutic relationship.

Tom entered into a whole new life of deep spirituality and great depth of human relationships. Throughout the day, he prayed not by himself but in the company of others. While driving down the street, visiting the grocery store, talking with friends in church, he prayed. He uttered the name of Jesus throughout his day. During his special times of quiet prayer, he now felt the loving embrace of the Father. All day long he felt close to God, since he now allowed himself to be close to people. A heart of stone, riddled with evil despair, had been delivered out of the clutches of Satan and into the warmth and reality of a loving God and loving human relationships.

Blaise Pascal magnificently expresses the power of Jesus—the deliverer from evil:

> Jesus is a God we can approach without pride and before Whom we can humble ourselves without despair.

Deliverance from Evil: Domination vs. Tenderness

In considering deliverance from evil, Jesus stresses that deliverance occurs within the context of relationships. He emphasized, "Deliver us . . . " The gospel is a call to a relationship with both God and others that is supremely hallmarked by sensitivity and tenderness. This sort of nurturance cultivates spiritual and emotional health, and of necessity drives out Satan.

Jesus battled Satan head-to-head in the matter of exercising domination or tenderness in relationship to God and other people. Theoretically, Satan could have possessed Jesus had Jesus succumbed to him. Satan offered Jesus a painless, powerful, dominating, and controlling life. With the power of Satan, Jesus could have acquired material possessions, worldly influence, and most importantly control over people. Never would Jesus have had to suffer the pain of Peter's rejection that came as he heard the words, "I never knew the man." Never would Jesus have had to endure the betrayal of one with whom he had shared His life and ministry—Judas. All of this Jesus would have been spared had he given in to Satan's pressure.

The scriptures record, "And the devil took him up, and showed Him all the kingdoms of the world in a moment of time, and said to him, 'To you I will give all this authority and their glory; for it has been delivered to me, and I give it to whom I will. If you, then, will worship me, it shall all be yours' " (Luke 4:5–7).

Evil entices human nature in and through inflation. The devil led Jesus to a high place. He lured Him with the temptation of pride and domination over others, that He would be exalted above all men. The excitation and pain-free promises of Satan captivate the egocentric inclinations of human nature. Everyone, on some level, desires immediate gratification of all impulses, instantaneous happiness, and complete control of situations and people. Satan will, at some point in your life, tempt you with this and may in fact grant you your desire . . . for a little while.

The story is told of the man who already lived in heaven and was struck by the curious and sudden desire to visit hell. He approached St. Peter and asked, "If it's all right with you, St. Peter, I would like a weekend pass so that I might visit hell." St. Peter replied, "This is a highly unusual request, but I will see what I can do." A short time later St. Peter returned and informed the man that he had been granted a weekend pass to visit hell.

On Friday evening the man left heaven and approached the gates of hell. Satan eagerly awaited him. He opened wide the gates of hell and showed the man an incredibly enjoyable and indulgent time during the entire weekend. At the end of his visit, the man was amazed and enticed by the pleasures of hell.

The next weekend the man once again asked St. Peter if he might visit hell. Once again, St. Peter granted his request. As before, Satan treated the man to fantastic entertainments and amusements. At the end of his second visit, the man felt completely taken over by the attractions and allurements of hell.

Upon returning to heaven, the man immediately spoke to St. Peter and asked, "St. Peter, I have enjoyed hell so thoroughly that I am making a request to live there permanently." St. Peter ardently attempted to discourage him. The man refused to listen to Peter. So, St. Peter allowed him to return to hell and permanently reside there.

Upon his arrival at the gates of hell, the man was once again greeted by Satan. The father of lies slowly opened the gates of hell, ushered the man in, and threw him into one of the deepest and darkest fiery pits in hell. The man was consumed with torment and misery. He shouted out to Satan, "Why have you done this to me? You always treated me so nicely before." Satan replied "Yes, I always treated you nicely, but then you were a tourist. Now you are a resident and you are mine."

The devil promised Jesus power in this world, including dominion over others. People leave themselves prey to oppression or possession by evil whenever domination and power take precedence over tenderness and sensitivity. A person's life may be totally run by Satan as he or she lives each moment to satisfy an insatiable hunger for power. In such cases, human beings are wantonly discarded whenever they block the path to power.

A very charismatic preacher once consulted me because of his feelings of periodic anxiety and depression. In our first session he disclosed the dream of the previous night: "I was in a dressing room behind a stage. A young woman and I were sensitively and caringly talking with each other. Suddenly, a power-ridden woman ran into my dressing room and told me that I needed to pray rather than talk with this other woman. If I continued with this conversation, God's power would not be with me. I would not be anointed to preach. It seemed as if thousands of people were waiting to hear my message. I immediately gave in to the pressures of this controlling and enraged boss-like woman. I completely discarded, threw away my feelings of tenderness and sensitivity for the young woman with whom I was so pleasantly engaged. I now felt that I would do anything for spiritual power."

In a quite insidious way, this pentecostal preacher had bought into the lie of power and domination. It veiled itself with spiritual concern and ministry. Little did his congregation know that his genuine call by God was laced with the arsenic of satanic promptings toward the evil of dominating and overpowering them spiritually. Domination and power, whether interpersonal, financial, intellectual, or spiritual are devilish. Their branches may seem to spread toward noble purposes; the discerning point is whether the action is motivated out of a desire for domination and power or inspired by tenderness and sensitivity. One is satanic. The other is pure Jesus.

After well over a year of working with this minister in psychotherapy, we together witnessed a wonderful transformation in him. As he willingly confronted the evil that had gradually but definitely possessed him, his preaching actually became much more inspiring. Others frequently commented that his forceful manner used to detract from his message. Now, grace poured forth from his lips in a tender and sensitive expression of faith. He told me during one of our last sessions, "I was my own worst enemy. My anxiety and depression came because of my own selfish ambitions. It's something, now that I have forsaken destructive power-seeking, God's blessings abound even more than I could ever have anticipated."

Deliverance from Evil: Narcissism vs. Selflessness

[The devil] took [Jesus] to Jerusalem and set him on the pinnacle of the temple, and said to him, "If you are the Son of God, throw yourself down from here; for it is written, 'He will give his angels charge of you, to guard you,' and 'On their hands they will bear you up, lest you strike your foot against a stone.' " And Jesus answered him, "It is said, 'You shall not tempt the Lord your God.' " And when the devil had ended every temptation, he departed from him until an opportune time. (Luke 4:9–13)

Satan saved his most powerful temptation for the last. He appealed to Jesus' human tendency toward narcissism. Self-serving interests, egocenteredness, lack of insight toward self or others, and scapegoating all characterize narcissism. It causes the individual to feel that he or she is above humankind. At the highest point of the temple, the devil urged Jesus to give in to the urge that all of the universe was at his beck and call. Narcissism places the ego at the center of life, relationships, and spirituality. The motto of the narcissist is "my will be done."

Narcissism presumes that God's grace is available upon demand. Together with this, friends and family are expected to know and meet every selfish desire and demand. In a real sense, everything is thought to center around the whims of the ego. Such a person is frequently described as having "a big ego."

Self-reflection and examination are anathema to the narcissist. Insight into personal motives, attitudes, and emotions is completely out of the question. Since the ego reigns supreme, healthy introspection is considered not only unnecessary but is unconsciously terrifying. Narcissists scoff at psychotherapy and spiritual direction, considering them to be a waste of their time. All that matters is that nothing interrupt their schedules, plans, and objectives. They demand that everything be kept running superficially smooth, with all the façades of proper appearances maintained.

Whenever problems arise, narcissists scapegoat other people. They find someone to blame for each and every life crisis and catastrophe. By never taking stock of themselves, narcissists are convinced that other people need to "shape up or ship out." They blindly believe that their lives would be more perfectly happy if others would only be more perfect.

Allen had been practicing the Jesus Prayer for one year. Throughout the day he whispered the name "Jesus" as well as taking aside two twenty-minute periods per day to pray in quiet. The constancy of his spiritual life brought Allen to an unexpected realization. His unconscious ties to both mother and father had nearly wrecked his spiritual and emotional life.

In a vivid dream, he recalled the Gestapo knocking on the door of his home in order to arrest him for disloyalty to the state. He and a friend of his had been prospering in a business endeavor that greatly threatened the existing government. The dream indicated that the officials regarded him and his friend as potentially more powerful than the reigning dictatorship. The Gestapo intended to throw him into prison and, if necessary, execute them.

Allen and his friend decided to flee from these oppressive figures. They ran out of the house. They were swifter, more creative and agile than the government agents. In fleeing they retained their creative enterprise. They ran and ran to a high mountainous area.

Since we were half-way through the dream I stopped Allen's recollection and inquired as to his associations with the dream symbols. He quickly stated, "The Gestapo were just like my parents. As long as I did things their way, everything was all right. I had to follow the status quo. If anything ever went wrong, it was my fault. They had my life all planned out. I couldn't breathe. I couldn't have independent ideas or goals. I had to do things their way. It nearly killed me."

Allen was the scapegoat of his family. He did not conform to the narcissistic pressures of his parents. He fought to live his own life. As the dream indicated, he was a very creative and enterprising individual who, when allowed to use his own resources, prospered. In fact, in many ways, he was far more insightful and creative than his parents. This threatened the status quo of the family.

After a suicide attempt, Allen ran away from home. He finally realized that living with his family meant stifling his own personality. For Allen, the end result of this would have been emotional and perhaps physical death. The narcissism of his parents was evil. The evil within his parents had nearly destroyed him.

The dream continued with Allen and his friend meeting a wise old man. As they ran from the Gestapo, they arrived at the entrance to a forest. There, a very wise and old man approached them. He told them, "You must enter the land of the forest for two years and then you will see yourself clear and be free from this problem." Allen asked the wise old man how they would find their way through the forest. The wise old man replied, "You must wear these and then you will see." He handed Allen and his friend two pairs of glasses. Inscribed on the rims of the glasses were the words "Custom crafted— DeBlassie."

Allen emphasized, "That's why I'm here to see you. You know the inner journey. You can, if you are willing, help me on the way. I'm ready if you are."

This began a relationship that lasted approximately two years. Through intensive psychotherapy, we worked through Allen's pain and anguish. We also came to discover his unusual abilities and talents. We encountered God, the presence of the living Christ, in the depths of his soul.

Throughout psychotherapy he practiced deep prayer through the constant utterance of the name Jesus. This greatly facilitated our work. His emotions flowed freely. Dreams and images surfaced from the unconscious in a manner that facilitated growth and healing. Through the presence of God experienced in the context of psychotherapy, as well as in his daily prayer life, Allen was delivered from the evil of his parents' narcissism. Deep prayer, experienced via psychotherapy and the Jesus Prayer, transformed his soul and his life. The name of Jesus, indeed the presence of Jesus, accompanied him through his pain and into freedom as he answered the call within.

Deep Prayer

Deep prayer is that moment in which you are aware of God, knowing that God is always aware of you. Whether through compassionate understanding in human relationships, through the in-depth analysis of dreams, or through the disciplined practice of prayer, God's presence can fill and enrich the soul of every man and woman regardless of their state in life. Jesus in the now, experienced in the depths of the soul, unlocks life's secrets.

Perhaps the most enriching way to abide constantly in the presence of the Almighty—to live deep prayer—is simply to utter "Lord . . . Jesus" throughout the day. With the name of Jesus always upon the lips, God gradually but definitely heals and transforms the soul. Health of body, mind, and spirit flow from His presence into the human heart with every utterance of the name "Jesus"—so simple, yet so profound, is this practice of deep prayer.

I share with you now a holy story about the great secret of life that is unlocked through the practice of deep prayer:

When the bishop's ship stopped at a remote island for a day, he determined to use the time as profitably as possible. He strolled along the seashore and came across three fishermen mending their nets. In pidgin English they explained to him that centuries before they had been Christianized by missionaries. "We, Christians!" they said, proudly pointing to one another.

The bishop was impressed. Did they know the Lord's Prayer? They had never heard of it. The bishop was shocked.

"What do you say, then, when you pray?"

"We lift eyes in heaven. We pray, 'We are three, you are three, have mercy on us.'" The bishop was appalled at the primitive, the downright heretical nature of their prayer. So he spent the whole day teaching them the Lord's Prayer. The fishermen were poor learners, but they gave it all they had and before the bishop sailed away the next day he had the satisfaction of hearing them go through the whole formula without a fault.

Months later the bishop's ship happened to pass by those islands again and the bishop, as he paced the deck saying his evening prayers, recalled with pleasure the three men on that distant island who were now able to pray, thanks to his patient efforts. While he was lost in the thought he happened to look up and noticed a spot of light in the east. The light kept approaching the ship and, as the bishop gazed in wonder, he saw three figures walking on the water. The captain stopped the boat and everyone leaned over the rails to see this sight.

When they were within speaking distance, the bishop recognized his three friends, the fishermen. "Bishop!" they exclaimed. "We hear your boat go past island and come hurry hurry meet you."

"What is it you want?" asked the awe-stricken bishop.

"Bishop," they said, "We so sorry. We forget lovely prayer. We say, 'Our Father in heaven, holy be your name, your kingdom come . . . ' then we forget. Please tell us prayer again."

The bishop felt humbled. "Go back to your homes, my friends," he said, "and each time you pray, say, "We are three, you are three, have mercy on us!' "

Come with me now . . . utter the sacred name . . . "Lord, Jesus" . . . in this moment . . . and for eternity.

Bibliography

Adels, Jill Haak. *The Wisdom of the Saints.* New York: Oxford University Press, 1987.

Beecher, N. M. *The Medical Tribune,* 8 January 1986, 3 and 15.

Bucke, R. M. *Cosmic Consciousness: A Study in the Evolution of the Human Mind.* 4th ed. New York: E. P. Dutton, 1923.

Chariton, Igumen. *The Art of Prayer: An Orthodox Anthology.* Translated by E. Kadloubovsky and E. M. Palmer. London: Faber and Faber, 1966.

Clissold, Stephen, ed. *The Wisdom of the Spanish Mystics.* New York: New Directions, 1977.

de Mello, Anthony. *The Song of the Bird.* Garden City, N.Y.: Image Books, 1982.

Guntrip, Harry. *Schizoid Phenomena, Object-relations, and the Self.* New York: International Universities Press, Inc., 1968.

Hausherr, Irenée. *The Name of Jesus.* Kalamazoo, Mich.: Cistercian Publications, Inc., 1987.

James, William. *The Varieties of Religious Experience.* Cambridge, Mass.: Harvard University Press, 1985.

John of the Cross, Saint. *The Collected Works of St. John of the Cross.* Translated by Kieran Kavanaugh, O.C.D. and Otilio Rodriguez, O.C.D. Washington, D.C.: Institute of Carmelite Studies, 1979.

————. *The Dark Night of the Soul.* Garden City, N.Y.: Image Books, 1959.

Jung, C. G. *Collected Works.* Bollingen Series XX, ed. Sir Herbert Read, Michael Fordham, M.D., M.R.C.P., and Gerhard Adler, Ph.D. Translated by R. F. C. Hull. Vol. 8, *The Structure and Dynamics of the Psyche.* Vol. 10, *Civilization in Transition.* Vol. 11, *Psychology and Religion.* Princeton, N.J.: Princeton University Press, 1960, 1964, 1969.

————. *Memories, Dreams and Reflections.* Edited by Aniela Jaffe. New York: Pantheon Books, 1963.

Luke, Helen M. *Love and Virtue in the Age of the Spirit.* New York: Crossroad, 1987.

Maloney, George A., S. J. *The Prayer of the Heart.* Notre Dame, Ind.: Ave Maria Press, 1981.

Merton, Thomas. *The Secular Journal of Thomas Merton.* Garden City, N.Y.: Image Books, 1969.

Padus, Emrika. *The Complete Guide to Your Emotions and Your Health.* Emmaus, Pa.: Rodale Press, 1986.

Reinhold, H. A., ed. *The Soul Afire.* Garden City, N.Y.: Image Books, 1973.

Rollins, Wayne G. *Jung and the Bible.* Atlanta: John Knox Press, 1983.

Sanford, John A., *Dreams: God's Forgotten Language.* New York: Crossroad, 1982.

Symeon, Saint. *The New Theologian: Hymns of Divine Love.* Translated by George A. Maloney, S. J. Denville, N.J.: Dimension Books, 1975.

Ward, Benedicta. *The Lives of the Desert Fathers.* Translated by Norman Russell. London: Cistercian Publications, 1980.

The Way of the Pilgrim. Translated by R. N. French. New York: The Seabury Press, 1965.